David. P. Morgan.

# ANGLERS' LAW

## In England and Wales

# ANGLERS' LAW

R I Millichamp

A & C Black • London

First published 1987 by
A & C Black (Publishers) Limited
35 Bedford Row, London WC1R 4JH

© 1987 R. I. Millichamp

ISBN 0 7136 5586 0

*Acknowledgement*
My thanks to Bill Howarth for his comments
and help during the writing of this book
Figures 14(a) and 14(b) are
reproduced with the kind permission
of the Welsh Water Authority.

Typeset by Latimer Trend &
Company Ltd, Plymouth
Printed and bound in Great Britain by
Billing & Sons Limited, Worcester

# Contents

# Foreword

To appreciate more fully, and to obtain greater details on, some of the subject matter in this book the following publications are recommended as additional reading matter:

*Theft Act, 1968* (H.M.S.O.)

*Control of Pollution Act, 1974* (H.M.S.O.)

*Salmon and Freshwater Fisheries Act, 1975* (H.M.S.O.)

*Police and Criminal Evidence Act, 1984* (H.M.S.O.)

*Salmon Act, 1986* (H.M.S.O.)

Stones Justices Manual
(Butterworth & Co. (Publishers) Ltd.
and
Shaw & Sons Ltd.)

M. Lloyd Parry, *Fishery Law* (Institute of Fisheries Management, 1976)

Michael Gregory, *Angling and the Law* (Charles Knight, 1974)

A. S. Wisdom, *Law of Rivers and Watercourses* (Shaw and Sons London, 1979)

W. Howarth, *Freshwater Fishery Law* (Financial Training Publications, 1987)

# Introduction

During the thirty or so years in which I have been involved with the enforcement of fishery law, it has become apparent that many anglers have but a sketchy knowledge of the subject which has led, all too frequently, to an encounter with a bailiff or keeper and to some form of legal retribution! Only in the minority of cases have anglers, as opposed to poachers, made a deliberate attempt to flout authority – the most frequent cause of their transgression has been carelessness or ignorance.

In an attempt to help rectify this situation I have brought together, under broad headings, some of the hundreds of questions that over the years I have been asked about the subject together with the answers which, as far as possible, are presented in simple non-legal terms. This creates a difficulty as, by paraphrasing some of the legal terminology, there is a possibility that some of the original meaning and interpretation will be lost. I hope, however, that the intentions will be clear.

The fishery laws of Great Britain and Northern Ireland have evolved over many centuries: in the process they have safeguarded local interests, protected ancient rights, met changing circumstances and continued tradition. These, however, vary from area to area and have given rise to regional differences that extend into present day legislation and the common law. Thus Scottish law and that of Northern Ireland differ in many respects from that of England and Wales.

This book deals with the law as it applies to England and Wales only. In many ways it is regrettable that there is no common approach to the law throughout the country, because there are many admirable features to be found in each of the codes that are lacking in the others; the combining of the best elements of each into a modern unified statute could prove of great benefit.

Most of the legislation referred to relates to the Theft Act, 1968, and Salmon and Freshwater Fisheries Act, 1975. Where it is deemed desirable to quote the wording of the appropriate sections of these Acts this is presented in a diagrammatic form which, where possible and for the sake of clarity, omits references to activities other than angling.

Many of the questions posed can only be answered in general terms – each case is different; therefore, the reader should not accept the text as the final answer to a particular problem, especially if litigation is envisaged (when professional advice should be sought), but rather as a guide to help prevent the law being broken by anglers and to assist fishery owners and tenants in protecting their rights.

# 1
# Fishery law

## General

If an individual wants to find out about the law relating to the
*ownership* of fishing rights, either on inland waters or along the sea
shore, he will not find the answers in any Act of Parliament because
these subjects have never been formally incorporated in any legislation – instead, they have evolved over many centuries as a result of
decisions arrived at by the courts. This is still going on and will
continue to do so, with the result that a present-day court decision
can overturn previous rulings of an inferior court on a particular
subject and that decision will hold good until such time as it, in turn,
is superseded or amended by a later decision of a superior court. This
whole process is the basis of our Common Law.

Occasionally, an Act of Parliament will be passed which deals,
amongst other things, with the *protection* of the rights of fishery
owners and their property; such an Act is the Theft Act, 1968, which
deals in part with the unlawful taking of fish.

The protection of the country's fisheries' resources and the control
of those who exploit them is contained in a number of Acts of
Parliament, or Statutes, the principal one relating to freshwater
being the Salmon and Freshwater Fisheries Act, 1975 – hereafter
referred to as "The 1975 Act". This Act is the latest in a long line of
legislation going back over many hundreds of years, the earliest of
which were concerned with removing obstructions to fish and
banning fishing at weekends. These two considerations have

survived through the centuries and are still included in the current legislation.

In the intervening period many attempts have been made to update the law to take into account changes in needs and attitudes. All have met with varying degrees of success and all have revealed weaknesses due largely to compromise, political expediency and bad drafting that later legislation has attempted to rectify. The 1975 Act continues the process by consolidating previous Acts but, like its predecessors, it too has its faults.

Scottish law differs in many respects from that south of the Border, although recently, in an attempt to control poaching which knows no such boundaries, the Salmon Act, 1986 has been passed. This includes provisions that affect Scotland, England and Wales but it, too, has its shortcomings and only time will tell if it achieves what it has set out to do. Little in this Act has any direct bearing on angling activities, apart from restrictions upon the sale and possession of salmon and the strengthening of the powers of the Magistrates' Courts to include imprisonment for certain offences.

The 1975 Act deals with salmon and freshwater fisheries in the widest sense and covers the protection of the resource and the control of its exploitation (see Appendix A). Angling comes under the latter heading but the provisions which affect it form a very small part of the whole Act. Nevertheless, from the sporting point of view this is of prime importance and, consequently, it is the only part of the Act which is dealt with in this book.

The enforcement of the Act is the duty of water authorities.

## Definitions

The Act defines certain words and descriptions that are liable to misinterpretation. These include the following, which are also used in the succeeding chapters:

"Byelaw" means a byelaw made under the above Act.

"Authority" refers to a water authority.

"Salmon" means all fish of the salmon species and includes part of a salmon.

"Trout" means "any fish of the salmon family commonly known

as trout, including migratory trout and char, and also includes part of a trout".

"Migratory trout" (sea trout) means "trout which migrate to and from the sea". Due to their migratory habits these fish are often linked with salmon in water authority byelaws.

"Freshwater fish" (coarse fish) means "any fish living in fresh-water exclusive of salmon and trout and of any kinds of fish which migrate to and from tidal waters and of eels".

"Eels" include elvers and the fry of eels.

"Owner" includes any person who is entitled to receive rents from a fishery or premises.

"Occupier" (tenant) in relation to a fishery includes any person for the time being in actual possession of the fishery.

All the above will apply unless the context requires otherwise when any change is specifically emphasised in the text, e.g. if rainbow trout are not included in part of the Act, the term "other than rainbow trout" will be used.

In addition, the term "game fish", which is not used in the Act, will be taken to refer to salmon, trout and char.

Penalties, when quoted, are those currently in operation either under the Theft Act, 1968 or the 1975 Act. These are amended from time to time – usually upwards!

An angler, in the context of this book, is considered to be a person of integrity who only falls foul of the law through carelessness or ignorance. A person who contravenes the Act under any other circumstance is deemed to be a poacher!

# 2

# Fishery ownership

## Who owns the fishing rights in England and Wales?

Ownership falls into two categories – public and private:

(a) *Public fisheries* exist in almost all tidal waters, i.e. in those parts of the sea which cover the coast below the high water mark of ordinary tides and in estuaries up as far as the tide may flow and, as the name implies, the public has the right to fish all such waters (see Figure 1). This is the general rule but there are exceptions that apply in certain places. These relate to tidal waters where, prior to Magna Carta, the king who then had absolute control over, and owned, the fishing rights granted some of these to favoured people in recognition of services rendered. Magna Carta put a stop to this practice by taking away the king's power to grant rights but the fisheries that had already been granted remained in private ownership. Being the property of their owners and descendants, these were disposed of as seen fit and changed hands many times, but their position as private fisheries is as valid now as it was when the grant was first made. An example of one such fishery is to be found in the lower reaches of the river Usk where a private fishery still exists in tidal waters.

Under certain Acts private fisheries can be created in tidal waters for the rearing and harvesting of different species of fish and such animals as oysters or mussels. Such a fishery belongs to the person to whom the fishery is granted under the appropriate Act.

(b) *Private fisheries* are found in all non-tidal and inland waters ("inland waters" are those parts of a river which lie upstream of the tidal limit in an estuary, canals, ponds, pools, ditches and reservoirs) and, as stated above, in certain specific tidal waters. The ownership of these rights can be in the hands of individuals, e.g. farmers, estates, angling clubs, syndicates, private companies, local authorities, nationalised industries or the Crown. All fishing on inland waters belongs to someone even if ownership is not at first apparent.

## Where is the boundary between tidal and non-tidal waters?

This is a question that has occupied legal minds for many years. The point at issue is whether the boundary marked the limit of where the tide ceased to affect the movement of the inflowing river or whether it was where the tide ceased to cause a rise and fall in water level. This need not concern the angler, because where a fishery adjoins tidal waters the lower fishery boundary, which should coincide with the tidal limit, should be shown on the deeds. The unattached angler wishing to find the boundary should refer to a $2\frac{1}{2}''$ Ordnance Survey map where, as a rough guide, tidal limits can be found marked.

## Where can the law relating to fishery ownership be found?

Most of the law concerned with the subject is Common Law and as such is not contained in any Act of Parliament (*see page 9*).

If a question about the law relating to fishing rights arises, its complexities are best unravelled by reference to a lawyer who is trained to delve into the Law Reports and precedents and to give an opinion based upon the facts.

# 3

# Public fisheries

**Can anyone fish where he pleases in a public fishery?**

Although the public has the right to fish these waters, the only way in which one can exercise this right without meeting some form of constraint is from a boat.

Fishing from the foreshore–that part of the coast which lies between high and low water marks of ordinary tides–often involves the crossing of private land above high water mark in order to reach it and to do so without permission could be infringing the rights of the owner or owners (*see Figure 1a*).

An example of the need to obtain permission before one can fish in the sea exists where a body, such as a port authority, requires an angler to have a permit to fish from its property.

Local authorities which have a coast line within their boundaries, and who control the foreshore together with piers and jetties to which the general public are given a right of access, rarely impose any kind of restriction on where people can fish, but they would have the right to do so if they so wished.

**Who controls the fishing in public waters?**

The fishing for sea-fish, crabs, lobsters and shellfish comes under the jurisdiction of local sea-fisheries' committees who are responsible for enforcing parts of the sea-fishery legislation, including the Sea

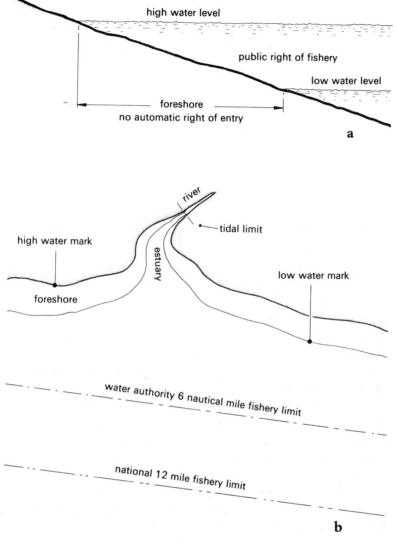

Figure 1

Fishery Regulations. The control that these committees exercise over anglers is minimal, but they do enforce minimum size limits in respect of certain species of fish – these vary from time to time and from area to area. There are also byelaws in some areas to control abuses by anglers, in particular the foul hooking of fish.

ANGLERS' LAW

The provisions of the Salmon and Freshwater Fisheries Act apply out to the six nautical mile fisheries' limit and are the responsibility of local water authorities. They cover anyone fishing for salmon, trout, freshwater fish or eels in tidal waters (*see Figure 1b*).

Between the six mile and national limits enforcement is the responsibility of the Ministry of Agriculture, Fisheries and Food.

## If there is a public right of fishery in an estuary, how can a club "lease" the fishing rights?

There are some places where private fisheries exist in tidal waters but these are very rare, and if a club has leased one it is very lucky indeed. A more likely explanation is that the club has leased the right of access to and along the bank or banks of the estuary. If this is the case, then the club can control the use of the bank for fishing by an unauthorised person, but this would not preclude anyone fishing below the high water mark – say from a boat.

If a public footpath runs along the edge of the bank, it does not bequeath a right to fish. A public footpath only gives the right for the public to pass to and fro along it, nothing else. If the land over which the path runs is private, but the owner does not prevent the public from fishing from it, it does not alter the situation: in law the public's only use of the *footpath* is confined to passing along it.

## Can one set nets on the foreshore?

As the foreshore belongs to someone, the setting of nets on it without the owner's permission would infringe the latter's rights to the soil and he could require the nets to be moved. All too often owners of the foreshore are unaware of, or are loth to enforce, their rights and this has led to a great deal of concern among anglers who turn up to fish only to find a net full of dead fish that have begun to rot or have been mutilated by birds. If the owners of the foreshore (of which the majority is presumed to belong to the Crown) were to enforce their rights, it would help overcome one of the big abuses of our fishery resources.

16

The use of these nets could be unlawful under Section 6 of the Act and if an angler has doubts about their legality he should report the matter to the local water authority.

## If someone catches a salmon in the sea when angling for sea-fish can he keep it?

If the angler holds a salmon licence issued by the water authority whose area includes that part of the sea in which the salmon was caught, and provided the fish was taken legally and in season, he would be entitled to keep the fish.

Should he not have a licence the correct thing to do would be to return the fish to the water, but human nature being what it is there would be a great temptation to keep it and if caught he would risk prosecution.

Some water authorities may be prepared to compromise if the capture of the fish is reported immediately – but it would be an unwise angler who relies upon this course of action without finding out the policy beforehand!

# 4

# Private fisheries

**How can an angler find out who owns the private fisheries in non-tidal waters?**

The obvious way is to refer to the local water authority, most of which issue comprehensive angling guides giving details of the locations of the various fisheries and the addresses of places from where permits can be obtained. If a particular fishery is not listed, it is probable that no permits to fish are available to the general public.

Other likely sources include the local angling community, estate agents, tackle shops, farmers and, in the case of canals, the British Waterways Board.

The absence of a notice board saying that a fishery is private does not mean that anyone can fish it without permission.

If the owner of a fishery cannot be found, it should not be assumed that anyone can fish the water.

**If there are no public fisheries on non-tidal waters, how is it that on some village ponds the fishing is "public"?**

This situation arises over a misinterpretation of the term "public". The fishery is not "public" in the same sense as a "public" fishery in the sea, but is public in the sense that any one is allowed to fish it without payment. The circumstances could have arisen due to the ownership of the pond being in doubt so that no one exercised any

control over it. An alternative reason could be that th⟨
the local council, wishes to let the villagers have free ⟨

Whatever the reason, the fact that no one exercises
not extinguish the owner's right, once his title to t⟨
established, to manage or dispose of it in any way he or she wishes.

These so-called "public" fisheries are not confined to ponds: they
can exist on rivers and canals.

Pond fisheries found on common land are not open to the public
at large but belong to the commoners – the local community with
ancient rights to do such things as fish, graze sheep or cattle, cut peat,
etc.

An individual may have a "prescriptive" right to a fishery, that is
a right established and acquired through longstanding usage. This,
however, cannot be exercised or acquired by the public at large.

## If a farmer who owns the fishing rights on a river decides to dispose of his farm, can he sell the fishing rights separately from the land?

Fishing rights are property in the same way as other interests in land,
and as such can be similarly utilized or disposed of.

In this case the farmer can sell them to one person and the land to
another. Care has to be taken, however, that the purchaser of the
fishery is given the right of access by an agreed route or routes over
the land, in order to reach the river, and the right to pass along the
banks in order to exercise his right of fishery. He should also have
the right to wade in the river and to do certain things on the bank,
e.g. trimming back vegetation to allow him to fish. It will be noted
that the person buying the fishery has bought no actual land but
merely a "right to fish and to take fish".

In some cases, as well as buying the fishing rights a purchaser will
also buy a strip of land along the side of the river, which gives him
control over other activities associated with the land that might
otherwise interfere with his fishing.

If a person buys land adjoining a river then, unless any fishing
rights are expressly excluded from the transaction, he is presumed to
have also purchased the fishing.

**If a fishery is rented, can the tenant get the same safeguards about access, etc. as a person buying the fishery?**

Many individuals and clubs only enter into an informal agreement with a fishery owner and this has considerable disadvantages compared with a tenancy based upon a formal lease drawn up by a professional person (upon which it is assumed hereafter that all tenancies are based), that safeguards the interests of both tenant and owner. What the safeguards are will depend upon what can be negotiated between the parties, but access to the river and along the banks will be a basic requirement.

Other conditions that should be sought by the tenant include the right to:

(a) trim back vegetation on the banks,
(b) carry out such works in the river as are necessary to maintain the fishery,
(c) stock the water,
(d) control predators, such as mink,
(e) remove unwanted species,
(f) limit the number of persons fishing,
(g) erect a fishing hut or shelter.

This list is an example of what should be sought; how an individual or club deals with a particular fishery will depend on circumstances and what he or it can get the other party to agree to.

The other party will also want safeguards and these will have to be agreed upon and written into the lease.

**Can more than one person own different fishing rights on the same piece of water?**

In theory one right, such as the salmon fishing, can be sold to one person and another, such as the coarse fishing, can be sold to someone else, but it is obvious that this would be fraught with difficulties, especially if both owners wanted to fish at the same time.

Such an arrangement is more often met in the leasing of fisheries where, for example, the salmon rights can be let in the summer to one party and the coarse fishing let to another in the winter.

## How can the boundary of the fishery be determined?

The deeds of the fishery, whether it is a lease or a conveyance, should have a plan attached to them on which the boundary of the area subject to the transaction will be shown.

If the fishery is on one bank only, then the boundary between it and the fishery opposite will be the centre line of the river.

The centre line of the river will remain the boundary between two fisheries even if, over the years, the river slowly changes its course, for as the river changes, so the boundary will change with it. Thus a plan attached to an old deed will not necessarily show the boundary as it is at the present.

If there is a sudden change in the course of the river, as may occur after a very heavy flood or as the result of major engineering works, then the boundary stays where it is and as a consequence a person who had rights on one bank only may find that now he has them on both, while his neighbour opposite loses his rights in part or in total (*see Figure 2*).

In certain circumstances the fishing rights may extend across the whole width of the river, in which case the owner of the opposite bank will have none.

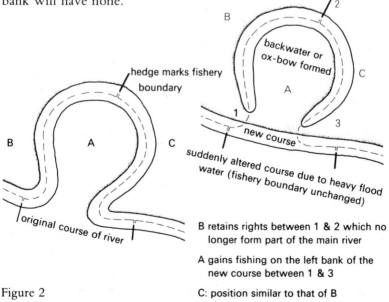

B retains rights between 1 & 2 which no longer form part of the main river

A gains fishing on the left bank of the new course between 1 & 3

Figure 2            C: position similar to that of B

## How do you differentiate between one river bank and the other?

Old deeds used terms such as "the north bank", "the bank in the Parish of . . .", etc. in reference to one bank of a fishery. This means of identification works where the length of the fishery in question is small but cannot be used as a general method of identification. If the river makes a 180 degree turn, the north bank becomes the south, and vice versa, while a parish may border the river for only a few hundred yards.

Current practice uses the terms "left" bank and "right" bank, established when facing downstream; this can be used accurately in whichever direction the river is flowing.

## If a permit allows fishing from one bank only and someone else owns the rights on the other bank, can an angler fish over the whole width of the river?

Until recently it was thought that, strictly according to the law, an angler could only fish in his own half of the river, but there was usually a mutually acceptable arrangement between the owners of both banks that each could fish the whole width of the water, provided they did so from their own half of the river. A recent Scottish court ruling recognised this commonsensical approach and decided that henceforth it should apply generally in Scotland. However, its validity south of the Border has yet to be tested.

It sometimes happens that, in order to fish his own side of a river effectively, the angler has to wade out into the stream. If he inadvertently, or deliberately, moved into the opposite fishery he could be committing a trespass, even though he was fishing his own water.

## What is the position about fishing off bridges?

If a public road or footpath crosses the bridge, it forms part of the highway and anyone fishing from it who interferes with its legitimate use could be accused of obstructing the highway.

A bridge which crosses a canal or river also crosses the fishing rights associated with the watercourse at that point; therefore, to fish from the bridge without the permission of the relevant owner or tenant of the fishery is an offence under Schedule 1 of the Theft Act (*see page 39*). If the bridge crosses the tidal part of a river, there would be no offence under the Theft Act. However, there could be an obstruction of the highway, and, possibly, an infringement of the navigation byelaws.

Fishing from railway bridges can be an additional offence.

## What are "banker's rights"?

This rather nebulous expression relates to the belief that where a person lives on the bank of a river he has a right to fish the water adjoining his property.

This can *only* apply when:

(a) the property adjoins tidal waters in which there is a public right of fishery, or

(b) the fishing rights form part of the property, or

(c) the property owner leases the fishing rights, or

(d) the property owner has a prescriptive right to fish through longstanding usage (*see page 19*), or

(e) the fishery owner allows the property owner to fish, or

(f) the fishery owner exercises no control over his rights.

Unless one of these conditions can be met there is no right of fishery for anyone living on the bank of a river. The same conditions would apply to a lake, pond, reservoir or canal.

Although the property owner may have no right to the fishery, the fishery owner may well have a legal right to fish from the property – even if this included the garden of the house. It all depends on the deeds relating to both the fishery and the property.

Where a fishery is sold but the land is retained (*see page 19*), the purchaser must ensure that he has access to all of the water, details of which will be included in the conveyance. Occasionally, through an oversight, this provision is not fully covered and the fishery owner finds that he is denied a right of entry across or on to land adjoining part of the fishery. Consequently, the owner of this land may consider that he has "banker's rights", but he would be mistaken if none of the above conditions applied.

## If a tow-path runs along a river, is the fishery private?

A tow-path along a river indicates a right of navigation which can be public or private, but this does *not* imply any public right of fishery, unless the river is tidal. A case in point is to be found on the lower stretch of the river Thames, above the tidal limit where, although the public have been in the habit of fishing for very many years without being required to have a permit, they have no right to fish. They do so "by the licence of the lord or owner of a particular part of the bed of the river, or they may fish by the indulgence or owing to the carelessness or good-nature of the person who is entitled to the soil, but right to fish as the public they have none". (This was the ruling in the case of Blound v Lanyard (1891).) If the owners of the fisheries can establish their rights, there is nothing to prevent them from making a charge for fishing or exercising control in any way they wish.

Even if the public is allowed to fish without any restraint from a tow-path, this privilege may not extend to fishing in locks or from weirs associated with the navigation. Special permission is often needed, frequently involving the payment of a fee.

Below the tidal limit there is a public right of fishery but no automatic right to fish from the tow-path (*see page 14*).

Where a tow-path is associated with a canal the position is more clearcut, as the navigation and fishing rights are frequently in the same ownership – usually the British Waterways Board – and the majority of anglers accept that they need a permit to fish these waters.

If the fishing rights have been leased or sold to a club, or other person or body, the use of the tow-path for navigation or by anyone for whatever purpose, with the permission of the owner of the navigation rights, does not imply that those uses include a right of fishery. This remains the exclusive right of the fishery owner or tenant.

# 5

# Interference with fishing rights

## What is trespass and what can one do about it?

Trespass is an unauthorised entry on to the land or property of others and is an offence dealt with under Civil Law. A trespasser can be asked to leave a property and, if he refuses, the owner or tenant or an agent of either can use *reasonable* force to eject him.

If a person suffers damage as the result of trespass, he can seek a remedy through the Civil Courts which have the power to award damages against the defendant and, in certain cases, may issue an injunction against him prohibiting the continuance or repetition of his actions.

## What is the position with canoes which interfere with the fishing?

If there is a right of navigation on the water, there is little that one can do about it. Such rights exist in tidal waters, on certain rivers like the Severn, Thames, Trent, etc. and on canals.

If there is no right of navigation and the canoeists have received no prior permission to use the water, then it appears that they are trespassers and can be asked to leave. Fortunately, the problem of conflict between anglers and canoeists, especially those belonging to the British Canoe Union and other organised bodies, is minimal. The major cause for concern is the unattached canoeist who uses the water without so much as a "by your leave". A similar situation arises with uninvited bathers using the water.

A circumstance that gives rise to difficulty is when the farmer owning the land, or other person with an interest in the land, such as a farming tenant, permits these activities to take place without reference to the angling interests. This can best be overcome at the time the lease or conveyance of the fishery is being discussed, when a procedure to prevent such an eventuality can be formalised and included in the deed.

**When fishing club waters, sport is often spoiled by the farmer who owns the land letting his cows wade into the river. Complaints made to him have failed to resolve the problem. What can be done about it?**

If the club owns or leases the fishing rights only, a farmer who owns or rents the land also has rights which almost certainly include the watering of cattle in the river. He may well have other rights which, if exercised, could also disturb the fishing and there is little one can do about it other than come to some arrangement with him whereby he agrees to limit his activities to times when fishing is minimal. It should not be overlooked that he may find some of the activities of the anglers equally annoying!

This shows that there is a need, when purchasing or leasing a fishery, for some recognition to be given to the legitimate requirements of other persons, who may also have rights associated with the water, as well as to those of the anglers. A well drawn-up lease will achieve this by the inclusion of a schedule showing what is required of both sides, arrived at by discussion and the agreement of both parties and which, when implemented, will allow minimum interference with each other's rights. If a breach of the conditions occurs, every effort should be made to resolve it amicably and only if all else fails should the aggrieved party seek redress through the courts.

If in any doubt about the terms in a deed relating to a fishery, one should observe the golden rule: "seek professional advice".

# If a fishery owner or tenant intends to carry out work in the river in order to improve his fishery, is he obliged to let anyone know?

Any work carried out in a river is likely, by its very nature, to cause some degree of disturbance to, or interference with, someone. It might even be illegal under the Control of Pollution Act, 1974 and should not be started without ascertaining the effect it will have both in physical and legal terms. Failure to observe this could have dire results!

Firstly, the water authority must be consulted. The river could be what is termed "main river" and as such any work in it must be subject to the approval of the authority. If it falls outside the "main river" definition (e.g. if it is on a small tributary), then the authority may still wish to comment on the proposals, particularly if the location is used by salmon or trout for spawning purposes.

The deeds of the fishery should also be consulted. These might show that the proposed work contravenes their terms and would preclude the work from being carried out.

The owner or tenant of the fishery on the opposite bank must be made aware of the proposals and, if necessary, his approval sought. If the work is to the detriment of his rights, he could make a claim for compensation against the person carrying out the work.

The use of heavy machinery in a river can discolour the water for several miles downstream and gravel loosened by the work can be transferred over considerable distances by flood waters; consequently, the fishery owners or tenants downstream who might be affected must be consulted as well, if such work is envisaged, as they can also claim compensation if the work either interferes with their enjoyment or has an adverse effect upon the holding capacity of their fishery.

Finally, make certain that all other people who fish the water know what is going on.

Any work carried out on any river, canal, watercourse, pond or lake without water authority consent which causes pollution could be a criminal offence under the Control of Pollution Act, 1974.

## What is the position if the water authority carries out works in the river to the detriment of the fishery?

The authority is unlikely to do any work – except in an emergency – which will affect a fishery without first discussing the scheme with the interested parties, which must include the landowner or tenant and the fishery owner or tenant. There is often a direct conflict of interests beween the two, for example where a farmer needs to improve the drainage of his land by lowering the level of the river. This can be achieved by dredging the river bed but in so doing the fishery suffers through the destruction of the habitat. These discussions can produce a compromise whereby, for example, the authority agrees to include in the scheme some work of specific benefit to the fishery, such as creating holding pools or carrying out stocking.

If no compromise can be reached and the work goes ahead, the fishery owner or tenant could make a claim against the authority for disturbance during the scheme and loss of capital value due to the work.

If a claim is contemplated, the fishery owner or tenant should be able to show that the income produced from the sale of tickets suffered because people were unwilling to fish in the conditions which existed during the time when the work was being carried out. A claim for loss of capital value should show that the fishery had suffered as a result of the work and that such things as holding pools, streams and lies which were essential for the maintenance of a good head of fish no longer existed. *To this end, every fishery owner would be advised to keep a log of the fishery in which not only catches but changes in water depth, flow patterns and bank configuration over the years are chronicled, together with a photographic record of its history.*

## What can one do about a person upstream who spoils the fishing by throwing branches into the river?

Section 49 of the Control of Pollution Act 1974, which the water authority is responsible for enforcing, provides that "if without the consent of a water authority, a person who cuts or uproots any substantial amount of vegetation in a stream, or so near it that it falls into it, leaves it to remain in the stream by wilful default he would be guilty of an offence" and he will be liable to a fine not exceeding £1,000.

If the culprit is known, and a simple bit of detective work examining the upstream fisheries should help identify him, speak to him and explain the legal position. If this fails to resolve the matter, then report it to the water authority.

Rubbish and branches of trees deposited in a river can alter its regime by causing gravel to build up and by changing the flow pattern. This can have various effects such as moving or filling holding pools, causing flooding, creating underwater hazards (resulting in fish being lost) and encouraging bank erosion – any of which will put a fishery owner or tenant to some expense in order to rectify it.

If the fishery suffered damage as a result of the rubbish, the owner or tenant could make a claim against the offender which, as a last resort, could be pursued through the courts.

## If the bank of a fishery suffers as a result of erosion, will the water authority put it right?

It is the policy of most water authorities to deal only with bank erosion where this has a direct bearing on one of their functions, for example, where the erosion is likely to interfere with flood prevention work or threaten a land drainage scheme. If a tree is washed down river and becomes lodged, causing erosion, an authority would normally move this if it was interfering with the flow of the river.

Where no water authority functions are involved, any erosion problem it agrees to deal with will probably be on a rechargeable basis.

## If fish are killed as the result of pollution, what should the owner or tenant of the fishery do about it?

Inform the water authority immediately by phone and arrange to meet one of its officers. The authority is responsible for the enforcement of the pollution prevention Acts and as such has the duty to investigate all pollutions, whether they kill fish or not.

An angler is often the first person to discover that a pollution has taken place and, as time may be critical, he is probably better placed to collect the initial evidence than an officer of the authority who may have many miles to travel to reach the scene of the incident.

If the cause of the pollution is seen, then you should take samples, in clean bottles if available, of the discharge and the stream above and below the point of discharge. Collect as many dead fish as possible and take a further sample of the stream from the area in which the dead fish are found (which may be a considerable distance downstream of the discharge) and hand these to the officer when he arrives. He will probably also require a statement relating to the circumstances.

If the authority has enough evidence, it may decide to prosecute. The offender, if found guilty, faces a heavy fine. Sometimes the polluter will offer to make some form of recompense to the owner of an affected fishery, but he is not usually required to do so by the court. Recompense may be in the form of a cash settlement or the restocking of the fishery.

Any action which the authority takes against a polluter does not prevent the owner or tenant of a fishery submitting a claim against him for any loss sustained as a result of the incident.

The numbers of fish killed will need to be carefully assessed and should include not only adult fish but immature fish, fry, the natural food of the fish and, in the case of a game fish river, loss of spawning potential. The total then has to be converted into a monetary equivalent.

Compensation for loss of income can be arrived at by a comparison of the income during the season when the pollution occurred with that of the previous two seasons – taking inflation into account.

Claims for compensation are rarely settled quickly so that an additional item in respect of interest accruing on the compensation money should also be included in the claim.

More often than not claims are settled after protracted negotiations between both sides, but if agreement cannot be reached the plaintiff, i.e. the fishery owner or tenant, can as a last resort submit the case to the Civil Court. If this occurs then it may be necessary to prove to the satisfaction of the court that the defendant had caused the pollution in the first place – which may be difficult.

Fishery owners, tenants and clubs can protect their interests against pollution by joining the Anglers Cooperative Association, which operates at national level and one of whose functions is to support its members in claims for compensation.

A claim for compensation arising from a major pollution affecting a number of fisheries is usually best approached jointly by all those affected.

**Recently numbers of roach and chub have been caught in a fishery which previously only produced brown trout. The coarse fish are believed to have been put into the river by another fishery owner. This has spoiled the trout fishing. What can be done about it?**

If the water was preserved as a trout fishery, it is highly unlikely that a water authority would give permission to introduce species that would change its character. To introduce any fish without the authority's consent is an offence under the Act (*see page 75*).

The problem here is getting evidence to prove that the suspected person was responsible. If such evidence is available (and the water authority should be investigating the matter), then the culprit can be prosecuted in the courts and can face a maximum penalty, if found guilty, of £1,000.

The change in a fishery which the appearance of an alien species can bring about may deter anglers who have fished there in the past from doing so in the future, thereby resulting in a financial loss. (This is particularly so on trout streams where the appearance of species like roach or perch can upset the natural balance of the trout fishery to such an extent that it becomes less productive and therefore less attractive to the trout angler.) If this can be attributed to a particular person, then the aggrieved party can make a claim against him.

The water authority should be able to offer help in removing the unwanted fish by using electro-fishing equipment or netting, but the chances of completely removing all the unwanted fish are remote and the survivors are likely to continue breeding.

## What is the position if a barrier is created in the lower reaches of a game fish river, resulting in salmon and sea trout being unable to reach a fishery many miles upstream?

It is unlikely that a water authority would permit this to happen, but if it did the upstream fishery owners who suffered damage as a result (by salmon and sea trout being prevented from moving up river) would have a claim against the person or body responsible.

The creation of water recreation areas in the tidal reaches of some rivers may involve the building of a low dam to impound the water and create a lake. Any such structure on a river containing salmon or migratory trout must, by law (Section 9, 1975 Act), have an approved fish pass incorporated in it.

Gauging weirs built to monitor river flows need not form a barrier, as most are so designed that fish can swim over them.

In the past power stations built in river estuaries have taken vast quantities of water from the river for cooling purposes and have consequently drawn in and killed many thousands of salmon and sea trout smolts on their seaward migration. In one case where this was demonstrated the electricity authorities compensated the fishery owners by building a hatchery to make up for the losses sustained and also developed a rescue operation each year which saved a large proportion of the fish sucked into the water intake.

Also in the past, pollution often formed a virtually impenetrable barrier to both the seaward and river migration of fish, but thanks to the various pollution prevention Acts and to the work of the water authorities and their predecessors, the river authorities, the problem has been largely overcome. Any new large scale pollution is unlikely if the existing legislation is enforced.

# 6

# Permission to fish

## What legal requirements are there of a person who wants to fish on private waters?

A person who owns or rents a fishery can, subject to observing the law, exercise his right to fish at any time and may grant permission to anyone else to do likewise. The permission granted may be free or subject to the payment of a fee. Conversely, anyone wanting to fish, but who does not own or rent the fishery, must first seek and obtain the permission of the owner or tenant.

The angler will also need a current and valid water authority fishing licence, purchased before he starts to fish (*see pages 45ff*).

## What is the difference between a permit and a licence?

*A fishing permit*

(a) is issued by a fishery owner or tenant;
(b) is non-statutory – it merely provides proof of entitlement to fish;
(c) is only valid for a specified fishery;
(d) usually entitles the holder to take all species of fish;

*A fishing licence*

(a) is issued by a water authority;
(b) is a statutory requirement;
(c) applies to the whole or part of an authority's area;
(d) is valid only for those species of fish shown;

(e) may have to be produced on request to a constable or a fishery owner;

(f) is not a substitute for a fishing licence.

(e) must be produced to a water bailiff, constable or other licence holder on demand;

(f) can only be used where the holder has permission to fish.

## What does a permit look like?

The following is an example of a typical permit:

---

**COPPER BEECH ANGLING CLUB**

This permit authorises:–

Mr ..............................................................................

Address .........................................................................

.................................................................................

to fish, subject to the Rules, Club waters for the period of:–

.................................................................................

ending on and including the .......... day of .......... 198..

Fee paid ....... Date ....... Time .... a.m./p.m.

.................................................................. Issuing Agent

---

This example contains the main elements found in most permits, i.e. the name and address of the angler, the waters he can fish, the period and date(s) to which the permit applies, the fee paid, the name of the issuing agent and the date and time of issue.

If, when purchasing the permit, you find that the club rules are not printed on it, it is advisable to ask the issuing agent for a copy or at least for details of the principal rules which apply.

## From where can permits be obtained?

Where a fishery is available to the general public permission to fish is obtained by buying a fishing permit. These may be obtained from the fishery owner or tenant, or their agents, e.g. fishing tackle shops, post offices, etc. In addition to selling permits, the agents are usually in a position to supply information about the fishery. The permit should be purchased before the angler starts to fish, although on some waters controlled by clubs a permit can be bought on the bank from a club official or keeper. The weakness of this system is that an angler will not buy a permit unless he is seen – if he is not, the club loses money. This practice is now falling into disuse.

Permits are issued subject to the rules of the fishery being observed and the conditions on which one fishes are contained in the permission granted. These are either printed on the permit or issued separately, and failure to observe them could have serious consequences for the angler (*see pages 42–3*).

## Can a permit issued to one person be used by another?

It is generally accepted that permits are non-transferable and on some fisheries the practice is expressly prohibited by the rules.

There can be exceptions, as in the case of an angler who takes out a permit in advance of going fishing only to find that he is unable to get there on the day. In such a case a telephone call to the fishery will usually result in his being allowed to transfer the permit to a nominated person.

## What happens if a person fishes without getting permission?

An offence under Schedule 1 of the Theft Act, 1968 will have been committed and if caught and prosecuted the culprit would, on conviction, be liable to a fine and the forfeiture of anything used in the committing of the offence (*see page 39*). Note that any person can seize the rod and line, which can be subject to confiscation by the court, if he has reasonable cause for suspecting that a person is fishing unlawfully.

Anyone who claims that he did not know that a fishery was private is unlikely to receive much sympathy from a court.

The absence of a "Private Fishing" sign does not imply a right to fish by the general public, although many brought before the courts

give the excuse that they thought they could fish as there was no sign
saying that they could not!

## Who is entitled to inspect a permit?

The permit is proof of the angler's lawful authority to fish on a
particular fishery. Anyone having an interest in the fishery, e.g. a
keeper employed by the club to look after its interests, a club
member or another angler holding a valid permit who suspects that
someone is fishing without permission, is entitled to ask to inspect
his permit. This power to inspect permits should be included in the
fishery rules.

A constable who suspects a person of fishing without permission
may require proof of his right to fish and this can be provided by the
production of the permit.

On some reservoirs owned by water companies and water
authorities the fishery may operate under a "general licence"
whereby any angler fishing is covered by it and need not have an
individual rod licence. The permit then is not only proof of a right
to fish but also proof that the angler is licensed and can be demanded
for inspection by a water bailiff. A variation of this can arise when
the fishery does not issue a separate rod licence but endorses the
permit to the effect that a licence fee has been paid. Again, the permit
is also proof that the angler is licensed and is subject to inspection by
a water bailiff.

## Does a club keeper have any special legal powers?

In his capacity of looking after club interests and as agent of the
owner or tenant a keeper has the power to require trespassers to
leave and to use reasonable force to eject them if they refuse (*see page
25*). If he holds a water authority licence he can, if he produces it,
demand to see the licence of any angler on the fishery and require
him to give his name and address. If anyone fails to comply with this
request, he would be guilty of an offence under the Salmon and
Freshwater Fisheries Act.

As an ordinary member of the public he has the power under Schedule 1 of the Theft Act, 1968 to arrest anyone fishing unlawfully on the fishery (this does not apply to anyone fishing with a rod and line during daylight) and to seize the rod and line or anything else being used to commit the offence (*see page 39*). *However, an arrest should not be made unless the keeper knows how to set about it – and then only as a last resort. Misuse of the power could result in a charge of assault or unlawful arrest being laid against the person making the arrest.*

Water authorities also appoint certain keepers and other individuals as honorary bailiffs. They are issued with a warrant which they must produce when exercising their powers; these are the same as those of any full-time water bailiff, and relate only to offences committed under the Salmon and Freshwater Fisheries Act, 1975. (*See pages 88ff.*)

## Does a keeper need to have any identification document?

Anyone required to exercise authority on behalf of someone else should be able to substantiate who he is and who he represents. His club or employer should provide an identity card. If he is an honorary water bailiff he should have a warrant.

Conversely, an angler should make it a matter of policy always to check the credentials of anyone he does not know who purports to be acting on behalf of a fishery owner or tenant and should always ask for proof of identity when required to produce a permit or licence.

*Be warned – never pay anyone on the river bank for a permit to fish, or hand over anything to a person who says that he is seizing it as evidence, unless he can provide proof of his identity, and always insist on a receipt for anything which is handed over.*

However, it will be seen later (*see page 39*) that under the provisions of the Theft Act, 1968 any member of the public can seize anything used in committing an offence under that Act. Such a person may well *not* have any written form of identity or authority. If this situation arises, the angler from whom it is proposed to seize the tackle would be advised not to hand it over immediately but to accompany his accuser to a police station and hand it over there, in exchange for a receipt, in the presence of a police officer.

# 7

# Ownership and theft of fish

## Who owns the fish in our rivers and ponds?

Ownership depends upon the type of water in which the fish are found. Enclosed waters owned by a single person which are isolated from a river system are treated differently from those which are not.

In the case of a pond or lake which forms part of an estate, and which does not connect to a river or stream, the land surrounding the water, the land under the water, the water itself and all fish found in it belong to the owner of the estate. (Fish farm holding ponds and stews, and garden ponds, are usually considered in the same way.) If the fishing rights or property is sold then, unless there is a contrary arrangement, ownership of the fish will pass to the purchaser. As the fish are deemed to belong to someone they are capable of being stolen.

Fish that live in running waters or waters such as canals and lakes which are integrated with, or are connected to, a river system are considered to be wild creatures which belong to no one. If these waters are stocked by the owner or tenant of the fishery the fish, once released, are deemed to have been released into the wild and thereby become wild creatures which belong to no one! However, once a fish has been caught it becomes the property of the person catching it – even if that person has no right to be fishing on the water. If he takes the fish away, he cannot be accused of theft as the fish belonged to no one and, as a general rule, one cannot steal anything which has no owner.

## How does the law protect the interests of those who own or lease fisheries in both of the above circumstances?

Where ownership of the fish can be proved then any person who takes them without permission will have committed theft, which is an offence under the Theft Act, 1968. Section 1(1) of this act defines theft as "the dishonest appropriation of property belonging to another with the intention of permanently depriving the other of it, and a person found guilty of theft will, on conviction on indictment (in a crown court), be liable to a term of imprisonment not exceeding ten years."

The offence can also be dealt with by a magistrates' court whose sentencing powers are not as wide as those of the higher court – although it can send a defendant whom it has found guilty of the offence to the crown court for sentence if it is of the opinion that the nature or magnitude of the offence merits a heavier penalty than it is able to award.

In most cases involving the theft of fish the matter is referred to the police who investigate the offence and prosecute the offender.

The unlawful taking of fish from waters in which they are deemed to be wild creatures is treated less seriously under the Theft Act. This is probably because no one is being deprived of his property, although property rights are being infringed (*see page 19*). Consequently, the offence is not dealt with in the main body of the Act but in Schedule 1(2). This states that a person who unlawfully (e.g. without permission) takes or destroys, or attempts to take or destroy, any fish in water which is private property or in which there is a private right of fishery shall, on conviction, be liable to a maximum fine, which is currently £400. If the offence has been committed after a previous conviction for a similar offence, the offender will be liable to a term of imprisonment not exceeding three months or a fine or both. This part of the Act also gives anyone the power to arrest without warrant any person who is, or whom he with reasonable cause suspects to be, committing an offence and to seize from him anything which on conviction would be liable to forfeiture. (*See page 35 and Figures 3 and 4.*)

The law, however, takes a more lenient view of people fishing unlawfully by means of a rod and line during daylight (this is

# THEFT ACT, 1968

### Schedule 1.2(1) & (2)
(Taking or destroying fish)

Any person who

takes or destroys or attempts to take or destroy

any fish

in water

which is private property or in which there is a private right of fishery

shall on summary conviction
be liable to

imprisonment for a term not          or a fine not exceeding £400
exceeding three months                              or both

---

The above shall not apply to taking or destroying fish
by angling in the daytime

but

a person who by angling in the daytime
(that is in the period beginning one hour before sunrise
and ending one hour after sunset)

takes or destroys or attempts to take or destroy

any fish

in water

which is private property or in which there is a private right of fishery

shall on summary conviction be liable to a fine not exceeding £50.

Figure 3

# THEFT ACT, 1968

### Schedule 1.2(3)

The court by which a person is convicted of an offence

may order the forfeiture of anything which

at the time of the offence

he had with him

for taking or destroying fish.

### Schedule 1.2(4)

Any person

may arrest without warrant

anyone

who is or whom he has reasonable cause to suspect of

committing an offence
(other than angling during daylight)

under this schedule,

and

any person may seize

from any person

who is or whom he has reasonable cause to suspect of

committing any offence under this schedule

anything

which on that person's conviction

would be liable to be forfeited by a court.

Figure 4

defined as the period beginning one hour before sunrise and ending one hour after sunset), when on summary conviction (i.e. in a magistrates' court) a maximum fine of £50 can be imposed. The power of seizure of the rod and line applies in this case but not the power of arrest. Note that this only applies during daylight: anyone fishing with a rod and line at night is treated in the same way as a person using any other method of taking fish and is subject to arrest and the higher penalties.

It is not necessary for the offender to have caught anything for him to be found guilty – his mere presence on the water attempting to take fish is in itself an offence.

The court by which a person is convicted has the power to order the forfeiture of anything which at the time of the offence the angler had with him for use for taking or destroying fish.

This Act is an extremely valuable help to fishery owners and tenants as a method of dealing with unauthorised fishermen and poachers; unfortunately, many people seem loth to use it, believing that the costs involved in taking the case to court outweigh any benefit that they might gain. This is understandable in the case of the infrequent offender, but where a fishery is plagued by unauthorised anglers a firm policy of prosecution under this Act is a very powerful deterrent. The court can also be asked to make an order for all or part of the prosecution costs to be met by the defendant.

## Does a person who has a permit but breaks the rules of the fishery fall foul of the Theft Act?

When a person is given permission to fish, either verbally or by the purchase of a permit, he is usually informed of any rules or code of behaviour that he is expected to observe. The terms of the permit are paramount and in granting the permission the owner of the fishery enters into a contract with the angler whereby the latter agrees to observe the rules in exchange for the right to fish. If the angler breaks any of the rules, e.g. by killing more fish than he is entitled to, he is in breach of his contract and his permission is then invalid and he becomes a trespasser (which is a "civil" not a "criminal" offence) and as such can be asked to leave the fishery; if he refuses, the owner or tenant can use reasonable force to eject him. As a trespasser he is also fishing unlawfully and the provisions of Schedule 1 of the Theft Act apply (*see page 39*). This gives the power of law to any rules which the fishery might impose on those who fish and, if implemented, has a far more salutary effect upon an offender than his being banned from the fishery.

If a person is prosecuted under this part of the Act, he might claim that he was unaware of the rules of the fishery. To counter this it is necessary for all to whom a permit is issued to have their attention drawn to the rules at the time. Ideally, the rules, or at least the more important ones, should be printed on the permit. Failing this they should be prominently displayed at all places from which the permits are sold.

## Do the provisions of the Theft Act apply in tidal waters?

As stated on page 12 there are no private fisheries in tidal waters as a general rule and therefore the Act cannot apply (*see page 38*). However, in those exceptional places where a private fishery can be shown to exist the provisions of the Act will apply. Anyone stealing oysters from a (private) fishery in tidal waters would be caught by the Act.

Although the application of the Act to tidal waters is limited, it does apply to fish normally found in those waters if they venture into the non-tidal part of the river where private fisheries are found. Thus anyone fishing without permission who caught a flounder in a private fishery would be liable under the Act.

## Can fish caught by an angler who has a permit be kept by him?

If the rules of the fishery permit it, certainly he can. This would normally be the case on game fisheries where a bag limit might operate. On coarse fisheries clubs sometimes place an embargo on the removal of fish from the fishery and require anglers to return them to the water at the end of the day.

Some water authorities limit the numbers and species of fish which can be taken in any one day under byelaw.

### If a fishery owner puts up a sign saying that "Trespassers will be prosecuted", does it give him any better control over unauthorised anglers?

A sign bearing the above words means little in law. As explained earlier (*see page 25*), trespass is a *civil* matter dealt with in the civil court, whereas a prosecution relates to the *criminal* law. Therefore, it is not possible to "prosecute" a person for trespass.

If a notice is to be erected it should read along the following lines:

---

**COPPER BEECH ANGLING CLUB**

Private Fishing

Any person found fishing on these waters without the written permission of the above Club is liable to prosecution under Schedule 1(2) of the Theft Act 1968.

Signed:– Joe Bloggs
Club Secretary

---

The effect of this is to take the matter out of the realm of the civil law and to treat it as a criminal offence which is much easier to deal with.

If the fishery is on both banks of a river, a notice at the upstream and downstream limits on each bank is desirable together with one at each point where the public is likely to gain easy access to the water.

On a practical note, a notice board which is flimsily constructed is not likely to survive for long. Although more expensive, metal or heavy plastic notices are more economical in the long run.

# 8
# Fishing licences

## Why does an angler need a rod licence?

Although referred to as a "rod licence", this is a misnomer, as strictly speaking the licence issued to an angler does not license a rod: it licenses the individual to whom it is issued to *use* a rod and line, and a gaff, tailer or landing net as an auxiliary to that use.

Water authorities are required under the Salmon and Freshwater Fisheries Act to issue licences for salmon, trout and (unless excused by the Minister) freshwater fish.

Licences are issued in order to:

(a) raise income with which to finance its fishery functions,

(b) prevent unrestricted exploitation of the fisheries,

(c) keep a check on the numbers of anglers, and

(d) provide a means of identity for those licensed to fish.

Under Section 27 of the Act it is an offence for any one to use a rod and line for fishing unless licensed to do so by a water authority (*see Figure 5*).

The answer to the question is, therefore, that it is a legal requirement for the reasons shown.

## What fishery functions does the licence income help finance?

As a general rule licence income is used to:

(a) provide a water bailiffing force,

(b) monitor fish stocks,
(c) maintain fish hatcheries and stock fisheries,
(d) create new fisheries,
(e) reinstate neglected fisheries, and
(f) protect angling interests against outside interference.

## Can anyone buy a licence?

A water authority *must* issue a licence to any one who, at the time of his application, is not disqualified from holding one.

Disqualification from holding a licence for up to one year is one of the penalties a court can impose for a fishery offence for which a person is found guilty after being previously convicted for committing an offence under the Act.

## From where can licences be obtained?

In addition to issuing licences from their own offices, water authorities also appoint licence distributors to act as their agents, from whom members of the public can obtain their licences. These are widely dispersed throughout the area and include fishing tackle retailers, post offices or hotels. Where authorities administer the fisheries on their own reservoirs they also sell licences on site. Anyone going to an unfamiliar area to fish should obtain a list of licence distributors from the water authority beforehand.

Angling guides, published by water authorities, include the names and addresses of all licence distributors in the area.

## If an angler arrives at a strange location to fish, without a licence, only to find that the licence distributors are shut what should he do?

If he wants to avoid the possibility of a £1,000 fine (the current maximum penalty for not having a licence), he should not start to fish!

It seems strange that some anglers will go to very great lengths to

# SALMON AND FRESHWATER FISHERIES ACT, 1975

**Section 27**
(Unlicensed fishing)

A person is guilty of an offence if

in any place in which fishing for fish of any description

is regulated by a system of licensing he

(a) fishes for or takes fish of that description,

otherwise than by

an instrument he is entitled to use by virtue of a fishing licence,

or

otherwise than in accordance with the conditions of the licence,

or

(b) has in his possession with intent to use it for that purpose

an instrument

other than one which he is authorised to use for that purpose

by virtue of such a licence.

Figure 5

ensure that their tackle and bait are prepared well in advance of a fishing trip, yet neglect to make sure that they have, or can get, a licence, and water authorities and the courts have little sympathy for the angler who gives the excuse that "the shops were shut".

Don't rely on getting a licence from a water bailiff – they do not sell them on the river bank. If a bailiff comes across an angler who does not have a licence, he will probably issue the angler with a "ticket" but not the type which allows him to fish!

## Can one angler inspect the licence of another?

Provided the angler produces a valid fishing licence issued by the authority in whose area both are fishing, he can demand to see the licence of another angler. If no licence is produced, he can demand the name and address of the other person. Failure to produce a licence or a refusal to give one's name and address is an offence under the Salmon and Freshwater Fisheries Act and anyone so doing should be reported as soon as possible to the authority or a bailiff.

If an angler suspects that another is fishing without a permit, the demanding of the licence is one way in which the name and address of the suspect might be obtained – assuming that he has a licence.

## What if an angler has a licence but has left it at home?

It is an offence not to produce a licence to a water bailiff when he demands it but, provided that the angler can satisfy the bailiff that he has a licence and can provide proof of his identity, no action will be taken if the licence is sent to the water authority within seven days. Most authorities issue their bailiffs with forms on which the name and address of the angler and details of the incident and the licence he claims to have can be recorded. This also informs the angler of the procedure to be followed for the production of the licence. A copy of this form when completed is given to the angler and the original is sent to the authority offices (*see Figure 6*).

If the licence is received on time and is valid it will be returned to the angler. If the licence is not received by the authority within the stipulated period, the angler could find himself being prosecuted. This could also happen if there were a discrepancy in the licence sent in, e.g. it did not cover the species of fish for which the angler was seen fishing, or it was out of date.

It follows that if the angler is not to be put to considerable trouble in sending his licence to the water authority he should make sure that he *always carries* it with him when fishing.

## For how long does a licence remain valid?

Licences can be issued for a day, week, fortnight, month, year or season, depending on the water authority.

In some areas a day licence is valid for a period of twenty-four hours from the time of its issue and a weekly licence for one hundred and sixty eight hours from the time of its issue, whereas in other areas a day licence expires at midnight on the day on which it is issued and the weekly licence at midnight on the sixth day after issue. Licences can be obtained in advance and the date and time on which they become valid, which is entered on them, will be the commencing time for determining the period of the licence rather than the date and time of issue.

A "season licence" may be a misnomer in areas where the licence expires at the end of the calendar year. In such areas if an angler fishes for coarse fish through the winter until the end of the freshwater fishing season on 14 March (*see page 56*), his licence will expire on 31 December and on 1 January he will require a new licence to cover him for the rest of the season (and the rest of the calendar year).

## If an angler fishes for salmon and trout in the summer and coarse fish in the winter, does he need to have three licences?

A licence to fish for freshwater fish issued by a water authority only covers the angler for the taking of coarse fish and eels in that authority's area. A licence to fish for trout covers the angler for trout, coarse fish and eels. A licence to fish for salmon covers the angler for all species of fish.

A licence is only valid in the area or part of the area of the authority that issued it. If an angler fishes, say, for roach in a different authority area or different part of the same authority area, he will require a freshwater fish licence valid for that area.

# ANON WATER AUTHORITY

Warwick House, Ammanford Road, Wolvingham ZZ44 99AA

## LICENCE DEMAND FORM No. 45632

To .................................................................................

of .................................................................................

.................................................................................

Occupation _____ Date of Birth _____

Registration number of vehicle of angler _____

You were at _____ a.m./p.m. on this day found fishing for _____ at
_____ by a duly appointed water bailiff of the Anon Water
Authority and on being required to do so failed to produce your current fishing
licence or other authority to fish contrary to Section 35(3) of the Salmon and
Freshwater Fisheries Act 1975 (see extract below) for the reason stated,
namely _____

_____

_____

You are required to produce such licence to the Fisheries Officer at the
above address within seven days from the date hereof. Failure to comply with
this notice may result in prosecution without further warning.

Details of licence claimed to be held:

Duration _____ Species covered _____

Name and address of distributor _____

Approximate date of issue _____

Signed _____ (Water bailiff). Date _____

Copy received     _____

(Angler)

## SALMON AND FRESHWATER FISHERIES ACT 1975, SECTION 35(3)

"If any person required to produce his fishing licence or other authority or to
state his name and address fails to do so, he shall be guilty of an offence; but if
within seven days after the production of his licence was so required he produces the licence or other authority at the office of the water authority he shall
not be convicted of an offence under this section for failing to produce it".

For office use only

Licence received _____ Licence returned _____

Figure 6

# ANON WATER AUTHORITY

No. 3546

## FISHING LICENCE 1987
(Expires 31 December 1987)

Salmon and Freshwater Fisheries Act, 1975

The person named below is authorised to fish with a single rod and line for freshwater fish and eels during the year ending 31 December 1987 in all waters within the area of the Anon Water Authority, subject to the provisions of the Salmon and Freshwater Fisheries Act, 1975, close seasons and other regulations specified in the fisheries byelaws.

Name _____

Address _____

_____

Date of issue:– _____ Time of issue:– _____a.m./p.m.

Issued by:– _____ Agent.

---

### Notes

1  This licence is not transferable.
2  Anglers must obtain permission to fish in any water from the owner or tenant. This licence does not confer a right to fish.
3  The attention of anglers is drawn to the following byelaws which apply to all waters within the Anon Water Authority area:–
12(1) The close season for carp is the period between 30 April and 1 July following.
13  The use of live bait is prohibited.
14  The use of a gaff as an ancillary to a rod and line is prohibited.
15  The minimum size of fish that may be retained in a keepnet or removed from any waters shall be as follows:–

|   |   |   |
|---|---|---|
| a. | Roach | 30 cm |
| b. | Dace | 25 cm |
| c. | Carp | 45 cm |
| d. | Bream (Bronze) | 35 cm |
| e. | Barbel | 45 cm |
| f. | Perch | 25 cm |
| g. | Pike | 50 cm |
| h. | Grayling | 30 cm |

16  Not more than one carp or pike may be removed from any water on any day.

Figure 7

## Does an angler require a licence to fish in tidal waters?

Despite the fact that there is a public right of fishery in tidal waters an angler will still require a licence if he fishes for or takes any eels, coarse fish, trout or salmon in those waters (*see page 16*), because a water authority's powers in respect of the Salmon and Freshwater Fisheries Act extend out to the six-mile limit. This is a requirement that is often overlooked, particularly by anglers fishing around the coast who take eels. Conger eels are sea fish and as such do not come under the Act, but the common eel which is found in both fresh and salt water does. Fortunately, most water authorities do not enforce the strict letter of the law in cases where eels are taken in tidal waters, especially in the sea, except where they are found in the company of coarse fish.

On some rivers the tidal influence is considerable, extending for many miles inland and providing excellent fishing for many species of fish, including coarse and game fish, as well as mullet, flounder, etc. (which are classified as sea fish and therefore do not need a licence), in water which ranges from fresh, through brackish to fully saline. Here, the angler fishing, say, for mullet may well catch other species for which a licence is required and in view of the similarity of method and tackle used must be particularly careful not to fall foul of the Act if he does not hold the appropriate licence or is unaware of its provisions.

## How many rods can an angler use with one licence?

As a general rule an angler is licensed to use one rod at a time, even though there is nothing to prevent him from having several rods with him – provided only one at a time is being used.

Some authorities may allow two rods to be used under one licence for certain types of fish and where this occurs the information is given on the licence.

## If an angler has two licences, can he use two rods?

This depends upon the policy of the local water authority. In some areas the use of more than one rod may be prohibited by a byelaw. For a definitive answer you should refer to the local byelaws.

## Does an angler need a licence for a hand line?

Unless expressly permitted under byelaw, when a separate licence would probably apply, the use of a hand line is illegal (except in fishing for sea fish). A normal licence to fish with a rod and line would not cover its use.

## The cost of a licence varies with the period for which it is valid, but is there a special rate for children and pensioners?

Most authorities issue licences at concessionary rates for children and old age pensioners.

Children under the age of ten are deemed to be below the age of ordinary criminal liability and it would therefore be impossible to enforce the requirement for them to have a licence; however, most young anglers feel that a fishing licence is an essential part of their equipment and if properly trained by caring parents will insist on one! In some areas there is a special rate for children under ten.

Children of ten and over but below an age determined by a water authority will need a licence which is issued at a concessionary rate. The age at which a child ceases to qualify for the concession varies between authorities. Some make it the sixteenth birthday, others the seventeenth; if in doubt, ask the licence distributor. Incidentally, the distributor is within his rights to demand proof of the age of anyone applying for a concessionary licence if he has doubts about how old that person is.

Most authorities give concessions to old age pensioners and a few make the same arrangements for seriously disabled persons, especially on reservoirs where the price of a permit includes a licence element.

Not every authority gives concessionary rates on all of the licences it issues – some only give it on the longer term licences.

The concessionary rate is usually a straight percentage of the full season licence and this will vary between authorities, but the savings are in the region of thirty to fifty per cent.

# If a licence is lost, what should the angler do about it?

Notify the water authority who issued it, in writing, as soon as possible that it has been lost, quoting:

(a) its serial number,

(b) the species of fish it covered,

(c) the approximate date on which it was purchased,

(d) the name of the distributor from whom it was purchased, and

(e) how it came to be lost.

From this information the authority should be able to check that a licence had been issued to the person making the claim and to issue a duplicate. A small charge may be made for this.

It is not always possible for the angler to check the details of the licence with the distributor, as he may have sent in the counterfoils to the authority. It pays, therefore, to make a separate note of the licence details in case it should be mislaid or lost.

# If someone finds a licence and alters it to his own name, is it valid?

The licence would not be valid and if a person is caught using it, he would be guilty of a number of offences, including theft by finding, fraud and fishing without a licence.

# If a club or a hotel has the fishing rights on a stretch of river, does everyone fishing that water need to have a separate licence?

If the water authority is satisfied that a person has the exclusive right of fishery on a water it can, subject to agreement, issue him with a "general licence". This allows anyone fishing with the written consent of the licensee to do so without the need for an individual licence. The general licence only applies to the specified fishery and if an individual fishes elsewhere (e.g. on the adjoining fishery) he will lose its protection.

The fee charged for such a licence will usually be based upon the licence income the authority would expect from those fishing the water if no general licence was issued.

## If a club wants to organise a trip to another club's water, where different licences are needed, can it get one licence to cover all members' fishing on the particular day?

Most water authorities will accommodate clubs in this way but they do require notice in order to prepare and issue the licence.

The person applying for the licence would need to send the names of all those fishing under the licence, together with the appropriate fee, to the authority well in advance of the proposed visit. This person will then be issued with the licence and will be responsible for producing it to a bailiff if asked to do so.

For certain classes of people, such as the handicapped, a special rate may be agreed by the authority.

# 9

# Close seasons

## What is a close season?

This is the time of year when fishing for certain species of fish is *prohibited* under Section 19 of the Act (*see Figures 8 and 9*).

The periods involved are laid down in Schedule 1(4), (5) & (6) of the Act and are known as the *statutory close seasons*. They vary between species and between different methods of fishing, but as far as angling is concerned they are:

(a) for freshwater (coarse) fish the period *between* 14 March and 16 June following;

(b) for trout the period *between* 30 September and 1 March following;

(c) for salmon the period *between* 31 October and 1 February following.

During the coarse fish close seasons it is an offence to fish for eels with a rod and line.

There is no statutory close season for rainbow trout.

The close seasons do not apply to freshwater fish and eels in tidal waters.

## Why are close seasons necessary?

Close seasons are needed to provide a period during which fish can spawn without being subjected to angling pressure. In order to give the greatest protection to the fish at this time it is necessary for the close seasons to correspond with the period of greatest spawning activity. It varies from river to river and between species, and it is for this reason that the Act gives each water authority the power to set by means of byelaw its own close seasons, which differ from the statutory close seasons, to meet local conditions.

## Why is there no statutory close season for rainbow trout?

Rainbow trout are not native to Britain and do not normally breed in the wild. They do not, therefore, need the protection of a close season. A close season can, however, be set under byelaw.

## Why is it that anglers in some places can fish during the statutory close season?

There are four sets of circumstances which allow fishing during the Statutory Close Season. These are discussed below.

(a) The statutory close seasons only operate where water authorities have *not* made byelaws setting out close seasons which apply locally (*see above*). The dates between which these byelaws operate vary from the statutory ones (starting earlier or finishing later), but the duration of the period must not be less than the minimum laid down in Schedule 1 of the Act, which is:

(a) for freshwater fish – 93 days;

(b) for trout (excluding rainbow trout) – 153 days;

(c) for salmon – 92 days.

Although there is no statutory close season for rainbow trout, a water authority can impose its own close season, by means of a byelaw, which must not be less than 93 days.

(b) If the fishery is specially preserved as a salmon or trout fishery, the owner or tenant can give permission, which must be in writing, for anyone to fish for freshwater fish or eels, which are not so preserved, during the freshwater fish close season (*see Figure 9*).

If the fishery operates as a mixed fishery, with the freshwater fish being considered of equal importance as the game fish, there is an apparent preservation element for both and it could be argued that in these circumstances the owner or tenant could not give permission to fish during the close season.

# SALMON AND FRESHWATER FISHERIES ACT, 1975

### Section 19(2) & (4)
(Rod close seasons for salmon and trout)

Any person who

fishes for, takes, kills or attempts to take or kill

salmon or trout (other than rainbow trout)

with a rod and line

during the annual close season for rod and line

shall be guilty of an offence.

### Section 19(5)
A person

shall not be guilty of an offence under the above

in respect of any act done for the purpose of

artificial propagation or a scientific purpose

and also, in the case of trout,

for stocking or restocking waters

with the previous permission in writing of the water authority.

Figure 8

# SALMON AND FRESHWATER FISHERIES ACT, 1975

### Section 19(6) & (7)
(Rod close season for freshwater fish, eels and rainbow trout)

Any person who

during the annual close season

for freshwater fish (or rainbow trout)

fishes for, takes, kills or attempts to take or kill

any freshwater fish (or rainbow trout)

or fishes for eels by means of a rod and line

in any inland waters

shall be guilty of an offence.

### Section 19(8)
Sub-sections (6) and (7) above do not apply to:

(a) the removal by an owner or occupier, from any several (private) fishery where salmon or trout are specially preserved, of any eels, freshwater fish or rainbow trout not so preserved;

(b) any person fishing with rod and line in any such fishery with the permission in writing of its owner or occupier;

(c) any person fishing with rod and line for eels in any waters in which such fishing is authorised by a byelaw;

(d) the taking of freshwater fish for bait –

(i) in a several fishery with the permission in writing of its owner or occupier,

or

(ii) in any other fishery, unless the taking would contravene a byelaw.

Figure 9

The object of this provision is to allow a game fishery owner or tenant to improve his water by removing unwanted species. It also allows him to delegate this power to anglers, but due to the drafting of the Act they are not required to remove any fish caught and can return them to the water.

(c) Permission in writing can be given by a water authority for the taking, during the close season, of any species for scientific purposes and also, in the case of salmon and trout, for artificial propagation or stocking. This permission is rarely given for angling – it mainly applies to the use of nets, electrofishing gear, etc. (*see Figure 8*).

(d) During the close season for freshwater fish they can be taken for bait from a private fishery, with the written permission of the owner or tenant (*see Figure 9*).

There has been a great deal of debate amongst anglers and fishery managers about the need for a close season for freshwater fish. It is argued that as most fish which are caught are returned to the water the species are not in danger. No doubt the arguments will continue.

## What about fishing for eels?

Eels do not spawn in the rivers of Britain. They migrate to the Sargasso Sea – an area of the Atlantic Ocean between the Azores and the West Indies – to do so. They do not, therefore, need the protection of a close season.

The Act, however, places a restriction on fishing for them during the freshwater fish close season, mainly to give protection to freshwater species which can be affected by the activities of eel fishermen.

Some water authorities feel that this restriction places an unnecessary limitation on angling activity and have removed it, thereby allowing eel fishing throughout the year.

## What is the legal position of someone who fishes in the close season?

Provided that he fished under any of the four circumstances described on pages 57–60, he would not have committed any offence. If, however, he fished outside these, he would fall foul of Section 19 of the Act and any byelaws made under it, and would, if prosecuted and convicted, be liable to a maximum fine of £1,000.

## What is the legal position if a person fishing for coarse fish in the winter catches a salmon or trout?

As it is the winter it is the close season for both salmon and trout – to catch either during this period is an offence under the Act. Under Section 2 of the Act, which deals with the taking of unclean and immature fish (*see pages 71–3*), there is a proviso that if such fish are caught accidentally and are returned to the water with as little injury as possible no offence would have been committed, but such a proviso does not appear under Section 19, probably due to an oversight in the drafting of the Act. It is most unlikely, however, that any action would be taken against an angler who caught a fish out of season if he returned it to the water immediately.

A salmon or trout caught out of season could be "unclean" (*see page 71*), and to kill such a fish would be an additional offence to the one of taking the fish during the close season.

In the past many anglers who have caught a fish, either out of season or a fish which was immature, and who kept it rather than returned it to the water, have used the reason that they did so because the fish was deeply hooked and it had to be killed in order to remove the hook! This is an excuse not likely to be accepted by a bailiff or a court. It is far better to sacrifice the hook by cutting the cast as near to it as possible, and to release the fish back into the water with the hook still in it – most fish will survive this treatment. The loss of a hook, worth a few pence, is far preferable to a hefty fine.

## Are lampreys covered by the close season for freshwater fish?

There are three species of lamprey found in Britain, i.e. the sea lamprey, the river lamprey and the brook lamprey. Of these the first two migrate from the sea to spawn in the rivers and, therefore, are not caught by the Act (*see page 11 for definition of "freshwater fish"*).

The brook lamprey, however, is non-migratory and therefore falls within the definition of a freshwater fish and as such is subject to the close season. It is highly improbable that anyone would wish to fish for these with a rod and line because of their small size and lack of sporting quality.

### Are such small species as minnows and loach also subject to the close season?

Although of no sporting value, except possibly as bait, the so-called mini-species, e.g. minnows, bull heads, loaches, ruffs and stickle-backs, all come within the definition of freshwater fish and are therefore subject to the close season and, incidentally, require anyone fishing for them to be licensed.

The enforcement of the provisions of the Act in the case of the mini-species is rarely applied, except where it can be shown that the angler was using the excuse that he was fishing for them as a cover for other activities!

# 10

# Prohibited methods of taking fish

**Are there any methods of taking fish which are prohibited under the Act?**

Under Sections 1 and 2 of the Act certain instruments and methods of fishing, which could be applicable to the angler, are prohibited (*see Figures 12 and 13*) unless their use is permitted in writing by a water authority for a specified purpose. In addition, other methods or baits can be banned in some areas under byelaw.

At first glance it is not obvious how many of these can apply to rod and line fishing, but an examination of some of the prohibited instruments will reveal a close similarity between them and permissible instruments and tackle, the use of which are accepted as standard angling practice. What creates the difference is the method and intention of use.

**When is the use of a gaff, tailer or landing net prohibited?**

If a gaff has a barb on it, its use is prohibited at all times under Section 1 of the Act, and being in possession of a barbed gaff with intent to take fish is also banned (*see Figure 10a*).

The use of an *unbarbed* gaff (or a tailer or landing net) used as an auxiliary to angling with a rod and line (i.e. to land a fish which has been hooked) is permitted (*see page 45 and Figure 12*), but any of these

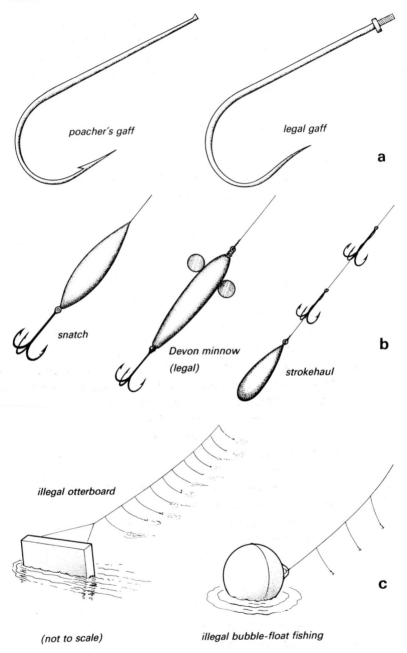

poacher's gaff

legal gaff

**a**

snatch

Devon minnow
(legal)

strokehaul

**b**

illegal otterboard

(not to scale)

illegal bubble-float fishing

**c**

Figure 10

instruments can only be used, in the manner described, by the person who is licensed to use the rod and line and has hooked the fish. Strictly speaking, it is an offence for any person, whether he holds a licence or not, to use a gaff, tailer or landing net to land a fish hooked by another person. Some water authorities prohibit the use of the gaff at certain times of the year, under byelaw, to protect fish which have spawned or are about to spawn.

## On some rivers anglers catch fish by foul hooking them. Is this illegal?

Section 1 of the Act prohibits the use of a "stroke-haul" and "snatch" (*see Figure 10b*). These are implements designed to be driven into the flanks or belly of a fish and comprise one or more large treble hooks mounted on the end of an angler's line to which a heavy weight is attached, either above or below the hook. The angler casts his line into a pool known to contain fish and recovers it with a series of sharp jerks, hoping that one of the hooks will strike a fish which will become impaled on it.

If a Devon minnow is compared with one of these implements, it will be seen that it bears a close resemblance and can be used in a similar way. The Act defines a "stroke-haul or snatch" as any instrument or device, whether used with a rod or not, for the purpose of foul hooking fish and this would include the use of any spoon or metal spinner in the manner described (*see Figure 10b*).

Anyone caught using a snatch or another item with the same function would, on conviction, be liable to a maximum fine of £1,000. However, if a fish was accidentally foul hooked, provided it was returned to the water with as little injury as possible, no action would be taken.

Many water authorities reinforce this section of the Act by a byelaw which makes it an offence *not to return* to the water any fish caught other than by means of a bait or lure taken in the mouth. This is often easier to prove in court and both carry a maximum penalty of £1,000.

## If a snare is prohibited, why is the use of a tailer permitted?

There is little difference in the construction of either – both consist of a loop of wire attached to a handle and both are used by slipping the loop around the body or tail of the fish, tightening it and then lifting the fish out of the water (*see Figure 11b*).

The tailer is only permitted as an auxiliary to a rod and line; if it is used in any other way, it becomes classed as a snare and is illegal.

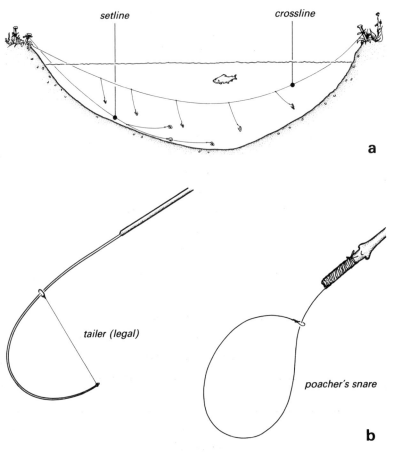

Figure 11

# SALMON AND FRESHWATER FISHERIES ACT, 1975

### Section 1.1(a) & (b)
(Prohibited implements)

No person shall

use for taking or have in his possession with intent to take or kill

salmon, trout or freshwater fish

any

| firearm | otter lath | cross-line | spear | light |
|---------|-----------|------------|-------|-------|
|         | jack      | set-line   | gaff  |       |
|         | wire      |            | stroke haul |  |
|         | snare     |            | snatch |      |

other like instrument

### Section 1(2)

If any person contravenes this section he shall be guilty
of an offence

*unless*

he proves to the satisfaction of the court

that the act was done for the purpose of

the preservation or development

of a private fishery

with the written permission of the water authority.

### Section 1(4)

This section shall not apply to any person

using or having in his possession with intent to use

an unbarbed gaff or tailer

as an auxiliary to angling with rod and line.

Figure 12

ANGLERS' LAW

# What other angling methods of taking fish are illegal?

"Setlines" and "crosslines" are also prohibited (*see Figure 11a*). A setline is defined as "a fishing line left unattended in water and having attached to it one or more lures or baited hooks". Such are often known as "night lines" or "bank lines". The definition, it should be noted, can also *apply to a rod and line which is left unattended* and anglers should be careful not to fall foul of this.

A crossline is defined as "a fishing line reaching from bank to bank and having attached to it one or more lures or baited hooks". It is unlikely that a crossline would be deliberately used by an angler.

Also banned is an instrument known as an otter board, which is defined as ". . . board, stick or other instrument, whether used with a hand line, or as auxiliary to a rod and line, or otherwise for the purpose of running out lures, artificial or otherwise". The otter board is essentially a poacher's instrument and consists of a weighted board that floats vertically in the water and has a long line attached to it in such a way that when the line is pulled the board moves parallel to the operator through the water. The line has a large number of lures attached to it, by short traces, which attract and hook the fish. It is most unlikely that an angler will go fishing with such an instrument, but he could well have a bubble float or like piece of equipment and this, if fastened to the end of the cast with the bait or lures between it and the rod, could be considered to be an otter board (*see Figure 10c*).

The use of any of the foregoing may be permitted by a water authority for the purpose of the preservation or development of a private fishery.

It is also an offence to throw stones or other missiles with the intention of taking or killing, or facilitating the taking or killing, of any salmon, trout or freshwater fish.

The use of a light for the taking of fish is also prohibited but the use of a torch to set up one's tackle, to bait a hook or to help land a fish is unlikely to fall under this heading.

# Are there any baits that are illegal?

It is an offence under Section 2 of the Act to use any fish roe for the purpose of fishing for salmon, trout or freshwater fish or to buy, sell or have in one's possession any roe of salmon or trout for the same purpose (*see Figure 13*).

The term "any fish roe" means exactly what it says and includes the roe of all game fish, freshwater fish and sea fish.

Salmon or trout roe, treated in a special way, is a most effective bait for some species of fish. The roe is at its largest size immediately before the fish spawn. This is when they are at their most vulnerable, since they have moved into shallow tributaries and headwaters of the rivers in order to lay their eggs. As treated roe can fetch very high prices on the "black market", its acquisition has led to poaching and, consequently, to the banning of its sale under the Act.

In some areas there may be restrictions on the use of some baits at certain times of the year as, for example, in the banning of the use of worms or prawns, when fishing for salmon, at the beginning and end of the season. This is imposed to give protection to unclean fish (*see page 71*).

Spinning for trout is prohibited under byelaw on some rivers where the practice is considered to be detrimental to the wellbeing of the stock.

Water authorities may also impose a ban on the use of hook bait or ground bait, particularly on water supply reservoirs, and the use of live bait, maggots, cheese, etc. is prohibited on other waters. These restrictions can be imposed under byelaw or, in the case of reservoirs, by the rules of the fishery. If fishing an unfamiliar area, it is advisable to check the byelaws for any local variations from the norm.

The sale of lead weights has been banned by parliament to protect swans, which die after eating discarded shot. Water authorities may extend this protection by banning the use of lead by anglers.

Clubs and fishery owners can make their own rules regarding the use of bait or method of fishing which, provided they do not contravene the Act or any byelaw, can be enforced using the Theft Act as explained on page 42.

The necessity for some of the restrictions imposed by water authorities is open to question and before any future restrictions are imposed the need for them should be established beyond doubt.

# SALMON AND FRESHWATER FISHERIES ACT, 1975

### Section 2(1)
(Fish roe)

Any person who

for the purpose of fishing for

salmon trout or freshwater fish

| uses any fish roe | buys, sells or exposes for sale | has in his possession |

any roe of salmon or trout

shall be guilty of an offence.

### Section 2(2)
(Unclean and immature fish)

Any person who

| knowingly takes, kills or injures or attempts to take kill or injure | buys, sells, or exposes for sale or has in his possession |

any salmon trout or freshwater fish

which is unclean or immature

shall be guilty of an offence.

### Section 2(3)
Subsection (2) above does not apply

to any person who takes a fish accidentally

and returns it to the water

with the least possible injury.

Figure 13

## What is an unclean fish?

An unclean fish is defined as "any fish that is about to spawn, or has recently spawned and has not recovered from spawning" and the taking, killing or injuring or attempting to take, kill or injure any salmon, trout or freshwater fish which is unclean or immature is an offence under Section 2.

The term "unclean" in the Act refers to any fish, but in practical terms it applies mainly to salmon and trout where the word "kelt" is used to describe a fish which has recently spawned. An inexperienced angler fishing a salmon river in the spring who catches a salmon should make certain that it is not a kelt as to kill one would be an offence. Kelts are much thinner than fresh fish and have ragged fins and "maggots" on the gills (*see Figure 14a*).

| feature | teeth 1 | gills 2 | body 3 | fins 4 | vent 5 | colour 6 |
|---|---|---|---|---|---|---|
| *fresh salmon* | small | bright red | rounded | unbroken | small | silver |
| *kelt* | large | pink | angular | frayed | large | tinny |

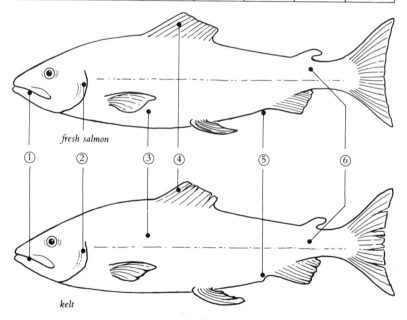

Figure 14a   Clean and unclean salmon

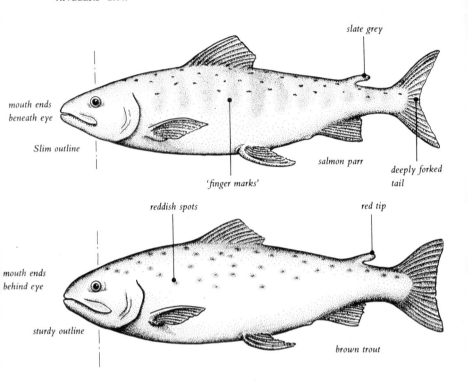

Figure 14b   Immature salmon and trout

As the season gets later both sexes of salmon and trout develop their reproductive organs, so that by the time they are ready to spawn the body of the female is filled with eggs and that of the male with milt ("hard" and "soft" roe respectively). A fish which is approaching spawning is known as "gravid". The question is often asked, "Is a gravid fish unclean within the meaning of the Act?" Fish with roe in varying stages of development can be caught throughout most of the season and if these were deemed to be unclean reported catches would diminish rapidly! An unclean fish is one that is about to spawn, so how can one determine if it has reached this stage? A very simple test is to hold the fish vertically by the head and *gently* squeeze its abdomen. If eggs or milt run from the vent the fish is unclean and must be returned to the water.

## What is an immature fish?

Section 2 of the Act also refers to "immature" fish, which are defined as "salmon of less than 12" in length, measured from the tip of the snout to the fork or cleft of the tail, and any other fish which is of a length less than that prescribed by byelaw".

The minimum size limit for each species is determined by the need, in theory at least, to allow a fish to spawn once before it is big enough to be caught. However, conditions can vary considerably between one water authority and another; so in one authority's area, roach may spawn when they are 7" long, whereas in another authority's area the fish could spawn at 8", and byelaws' size limits are set to allow for these variations. This method is not always followed but the principle explains the difference in size limits between one area and another.

The 12" limit for salmon is designed to protect the young fish up until the time when they migrate downstream to the sea – usually when about 6" in length – and is considerably lower than the length at which even the smallest salmon will spawn. The young fish which can frequent most stretches of a river have feeding habits and appearance similar to trout and are often mistaken for them (*see Figure 14b*). If caught by an angler they must be unhooked gently and returned to the river immediately.

## How should an angler measure a fish to check if it is immature?

The usual method laid down under byelaw is for the length to be measured from the tip of the nose or snout to the *fork* of the tail, but not all water authorities use this. Some require the length to be measured from the tip of the nose or snout to the *end* of the tail. The difference in length from the fork to the tip of the tail can vary from a few millimetres to several centimetres, depending upon the age and species of the fish. Thus an eight-inch roach measured to the tip of the tail could be taken in one area but the same fish, caught in another area also with an eight-inch limit but where length is to the fork of the tail, could not be taken.

## Can an angling club set its own size limits?

Provided that any limit set is not smaller than that laid down in the water authority byelaws, a club or anyone else running a fishery can set its own size limits.

## Can undersized fish be caught as bait?

This will depend on the water authority in whose area the fish are caught. Some allow small fish to be caught and used as bait while others make no concessions.

The use of small fish as bait may be linked to the practice of "live-baiting" which is prohibited in some parts of the country, so make sure that no such ban exists before taking the fish, otherwise they would be wasted.

## What is the legal position if an unclean or immature fish is caught accidentally?

The law recognises that both categories of fish can be caught accidentally and provides that the offence of taking such fish will not apply if the fish are returned to the water with the least possible injury (*see Figure 13*).

An immature fish caught and placed in a keep-net to be returned later to the water may not come within this proviso, as the placing of it in the keep-net could be construed as causing it injury. It should be noted, however, that some water authorities do allow this under byelaw.

## What is the penalty for using illegal bait and taking unclean or immature fish?

A maximum fine of £1,000.

# 11
# Stocking and moving fish

## Does an angler need permission to stock a fishery?

To stock any inland waters requires the consent of the water authority under Section 30 of the Act (*see Figure 15*). This is necessary to keep control over the movement of fish in order to prevent the spread of disease and parasites from one river or area to another and to help trace the source of any infection should it occur (*see page 30*).

Unless catered for in the lease, a fishery tenant may also require the consent of the owner.

## How does one set about stocking?

There are a number of logical steps to be followed if the stocking is to proceed smoothly. These are:
  (a) Survey the fishery to determine if the water is chemically and biologically suitable – trout, for example, from a hatchery with an alkaline water supply are unlikely to thrive in a fishery which has an acidic water.
  (b) Ensure that the species to be stocked are compatible with the existing population, i.e. do not contemplate introducing an alien species if the authority is likely to object.
  (c) Ensure that the fishery has the capacity to hold the new fish.

---

# SALMON AND FRESHWATER FISHERIES ACT, 1975

**Section 30**
(Introduction of fish)

A person shall be guilty of an offence

if he introduces any fish or spawn of fish

into an inland water

or has in his possession any fish or spawn of fish

intending to introduce it into an inland water

*unless*

he first obtains the written consent of the water authority.

---

Figure 15

(d) Make certain through preliminary enquiries that someone can supply the fish and get a provisional delivery date, but do not place a firm order at this stage. It is also wise to find an alternative source in case the first is unable to supply at the last minute.

(e) Write to the authority asking for consent to stock giving the following information:
  (i) number and species of fish;
  (ii) source(s) from which to be obtained;
  (iii) location and nature of water to be stocked;
  (iv) existing species in the water;
  (v) date of stocking.

(f) When the consent is issued send a copy of it to the supplier with the order.

(g) Inform the authority of the time when delivery is expected.

The authority may supply forms on which the applications can be made and an advisory leaflet on the best procedure to be adopted.

# Do you need to go to a fish farm to get fish for stocking?

Fish can be obtained from any source, but it is only from the recognised ones that a water authority is likely to allow fish to be brought into its area.

Some fisheries may have surplus stocks for disposal which others would wish to introduce to their waters. Provided that the above procedure is followed and the authority agrees, the transfer can take place.

# If a club owns fisheries on two different rivers, can it net fish from one river and transfer them to the other?

No fish can be moved from one water to another without water authority consent. If the consent to move the fish is granted, the club will also need approval to use a net with which to catch them – it would be illegal to use the net without approval.

If the club purchased an electro-fishing machine in order to manage its fish stocks, it would require consent under Section 5 of the Act. Under this section it is illegal to use electrical equipment, explosives or poisons to take fish, but consent in writing can be given by the authority (or the Ministry of Agriculture, Fisheries and Food in the case of the poison) to use these otherwise prohibited methods. Once consent has been granted the equipment may need to be licensed, for which a fee will be payable: this will depend upon the policy adopted by the water authority concerned, but would be obligatory if salmon or trout were being fished.

# What should one do with unused live-bait brought from another area at the end of a day's fishing?

Some authorities prohibit live-bait, while others prohibit the use of live-bait which comes from waters outside their areas. If in any doubt always check the local byelaws.

It may well be preferable to return any live-bait to the place from whence it came rather than dispose of it into a fishery if the angler is unsure of his legal position.

## How can water authorities move fish around so easily? Do they need to give themselves consent?

Under the Water Act, the Water Resources Act and the Salmon and Freshwater Fisheries Act water authorities have a number of statutory obligations. These include the duty to "maintain, improve and develop the salmon fisheries, trout fisheries, freshwater fisheries and eel fisheries in the area for which they exercise functions under the Act". This gives them the power to do many things which would be illegal if done by anyone else. However, they are required to comply with the common law (unless this has been over-ridden by statute for certain functions) and the Theft Act. An authority cannot, for example, remove any fish or the eggs of fish from a private fishery without the permission of the owner or tenant and even a scientific survey, involving the catching, examination and subsequent release of fish, needs this permission (*see page 39*).

# 12
# Sale of fish

## Is there a time of year when fish cannot be sold?

Section 22 of the Act prohibits the sale of:
  (a) salmon between 31 August and the following 1 February, and
  (b) trout, other than rainbow trout, between 31 August and the
      following 1 March (*see also exceptions below*).
  There is no prohibition on the sale of rainbow trout or freshwater
fish (*see Figure 16*).

## Why is there a need to ban the sale of fish at certain times of the year?

The object is to prevent the over-exploitation of vulnerable species
at the time when they are at most risk. In the case of salmon and
trout this is at the approach to and during the spawning season.
  Fish for which there is no great demand as food and which are not
vulnerable, at the current rate of exploitation, fall outside this
requirement.

## Why is angling allowed after these dates if the fish cannot be sold?

There are exceptions under Section 22 which allow for the sale of

# SALMON AND FRESHWATER FISHERIES ACT, 1975

### Section 22(1)
(Sale of salmon and trout)

Any person who

buys, sells, or exposes for sale or has in possession for sale

any salmon

between 31 August and the following 1 February; or

any trout (other than rainbow trout)

between 31 August and the following 1 March

shall be guilty of an offence.

### Section 22(2)
Subsection (1) above shall not apply to any person

buying, selling or exposing for sale,

or having in his possession for sale,

any salmon or trout (other than unclean or immature salmon or trout)

caught within the United Kingdom

if its capture by any net, instrument or device

was lawful at the time and place where it was caught.

### Section 22(3)
A person shall not be guilty of an offence in respect of trout

under this section

for any act done for the purpose of

artificial propagation of fish or

the stocking or restocking of waters or

for some scientific purpose.

Figure 16

fish, particularly if imported, frozen or caught outside the United Kingdom, during the times given above and which also apply to any salmon or trout (other than unclean or immature fish) (*see pages 70–3*) caught within the United Kingdom if their capture by any net, instrument or device was lawful at the time and in the place where they were caught.

This means that if a water authority allows fishing until, say, the end of September then any salmon or trout, which is not unclean or immature, caught by an angler can be sold.

## Why is there no restriction on the sale of rainbow trout?

Rainbow trout form the backbone of commercial fish rearing for food in Britain and to place any restriction on their sale would be an unacceptable imposition on an important industry.

Also, as they rarely breed in the wild in this country the need to protect them during a spawning season does not exist and so there is no need to impose any restriction on their sale.

## Why is there no restriction on the sale of freshwater fish?

As stated on page 79 above species which are not at risk and for which there is no great demand are not considered to merit the protection of the law. Freshwater fish come within this category especially, as food fish, although there is a demand for them as stock fish. Should the position arise where, for example, pike became an established gastronomic delicacy, leading to the over-exploitation of the stock, it is possible that a restriction on its sale might be introduced.

## Can anyone buy and sell salmon?

Until recently there were no restrictions on who could deal in salmon but, in future, under the Salmon Act 1986 anyone intending to deal in salmon (which includes sea trout) will need to be licensed.

It would appear from the wording of the Act that an angler who wished to sell his catch would need a dealer's licence. However, the minister has yet to make an order setting out how the provisions of the Act will apply and until this has been done its effect upon an angler cannot be determined.

Under the Act it is also an offence to handle fish dishonestly.

## If a water bailiff suspects that a person has bought or sold a fish during the prohibited time how can he hope to prove it?

It is a basic premise of the law that the prosecution has to prove a defendant guilty. There is an exception to this where it can be shown that the buying, selling or exposing for sale has taken place in contravention of Section 22 of the 1975 Act. In such circumstances the onus of proof that no offence has been committed rests with the person suspected of the offence.

If buying or selling fish legally, it is advisable to obtain or give a receipt to the other party, which can be produced if required. This is particularly important in the case of hotels, which will need a dealer's licence under the 1986 Act to do so, if fish are purchased from individual fishermen who are perhaps staying as guests. Such fish, if placed in cold storage and subsequently served on the menu after the season is over, could place the person making the purchase in jeopardy if he is unable to show proof that the fish were taken legally in season.

## What is the penalty for selling fish at the wrong time?

If found guilty, a maximum fine of £1,000.

# 13
# Byelaws and orders

## Why are byelaws made?

The 1975 Act has a general application in England and Wales, but conditions and circumstances are not uniform everywhere and consequently the provisions of the Act are less effective in some areas than in others. To overcome this there is provision for these weaknesses to be countered by byelaws which adapt the Act to comply more effectively with local requirements.

## Who makes the byelaws?

Under Section 28 of the Act water authorities are given the power to make byelaws which are subject to approval by the minister. There is a procedure laid down in the Act which requires any proposed byelaws to be advertised. Any objections raised would be considered by the minister who could cause a public local enquiry to be held to look at such objections.

Before submitting byelaws for approval, an authority would normally consult with the various fishery interests in its area and attempt to get a measure of agreement from them.

## How long does it take to get byelaws approved?

If there are no objections, the minister may approve them in as little as a month or two.

If the minister causes a public enquiry to be held, he will appoint an Inspector to hear it and report to him. The complexity of the evidence given and the number of objectors will influence the time taken for the enquiry to complete its hearing and for the Inspector to complete his report. It could take a year or more!

## For what purpose can byelaws be made?

There are eighteen purposes given in Schedule 3 of the Act for which byelaws can be made. Not all relate to angling but those that do include the following:

(a) fixing or altering the close season;

(b) dispensing with the close season for freshwater fish or rainbow trout;

(c) specifying nets which may be used, including keepnets;

(d) prohibiting the use, and time of use, of certain instruments;

(e) prohibiting the taking or removal of any fish whether alive or dead from any waters;

(f) prohibiting or regulating the taking of trout or freshwater fish of a size less than that prescribed by the byelaw;

(g) prohibiting or regulating the taking of fish above or below any dam or other obstruction;

(h) prohibiting or regulating fishing with rod and line during the hours of darkness;

(i) requiring anglers to submit details of fish caught;

(j) regulating the use of any lure or bait used in connection with fishing with rod and line;

(k) determining a time when the use of a gaff shall be lawful;

(l) authorising the fishing for eels during the annual close season for freshwater fish; and

(m) a better execution of the Act and better protection, preservation and improvement of the fisheries in a water authority area.

Some of these have been discussed previously in the context of their application to a particular subject.

The list is quite extensive and in (m) includes the means whereby an authority can do almost anything by way of byelaw, and subject to Ministry approval, to control the fisheries in its area.

*Note*  The wording used in byelaws by different authorities to achieve the same objective can vary considerably: some use a permissive format while others are prohibitive (*see Appendix B*) – this can be confusing to an angler who fishes in more than one authority area.

## What examples are there of byelaws made under the above?

Apart from those already discussed earlier, the following are frequently found in operation by one authority or another:

(a) The size, mesh and material of keep-nets can be regulated. This is to help minimise harm done to fish kept in them due to descaling and other physical damage.

(b) A prohibition on the removal of any dead or live fish from any waters other than by means of a rod and line can be imposed. The reason for this is to overcome the excuse used by some people that a fish caught illegally had "been found dead in the river".

(c) On game fish rivers salmon and trout congregate in large numbers near obstructions where they can be foul-hooked or netted. A remedial measure by means of a byelaw can be introduced to prohibit fishing within a certain distance upstream and/or downstream of an obstruction.

(d) On some fisheries, such as water authority reservoirs, fishing at night is prohibited under byelaw. This can also be imposed on rivers where night fishing poses a problem.

(e) Most authorities with game fisheries require anglers to submit details of fish caught, including species, weight, location and method used. If no fish are taken, the angler is required to submit a "Nil" return. This information is of vital importance in assessing the productivity of the fishery and revealing any trends which, if detrimental, can be countered.

Actual examples of byelaws made by water authorities are given in Appendix B.

## If an angler fails to submit a catch return to an authority or breaks any of the byelaws, what penalty does he face?

Byelaws are considered to be an integral part of the fisheries' legislation and as such are treated in the same way as the majority of the provisions of the main Act, carrying a maximum penalty of £1,000 for failure to comply.

If an angler is required by byelaw to make a return of any fish caught and he fails to do so, he faces a hefty penalty. The fact that he caught no fish at all during the season is not a valid excuse, as authorities require "Nil" returns to be made.

## How can an angler be expected to know what is in all the byelaws?

If he has any doubts before he goes fishing, he should get a copy of the local byelaws from the water authority. In some areas extracts relating to angling are printed on the licence, but if this is not the case it is no excuse in law. The angler is expected to know the law in the same way that any other sportsman is expected to know the rules of his particular sport.

## What is the difference between a byelaw and an order made under the Act?

Whereas byelaws *amend* certain sections of the Act to meet local conditions and are subject to the approval of the Minister, an order modifies the Act to allow an authority to do things not specifically included in it and is subject to parliamentary approval.

## For what purposes can an order be made?

There are three bases on which an order may be approved:
  (a) to provide for the imposition and collection of a fishery rate from owners and occupiers of fisheries;

(b) to enable a water authority to erect and work any fixed engine for catching salmon and migratory trout;

(c) to modify the provisions of the Act which relate to the regulation of fisheries. This gives considerable scope to a water authority and allows it to do such things as dispense with a close season or prohibit all fishing in certain areas.

# 14

# Powers of water bailiffs

**Are water bailiffs given any special powers and, if so, for what reason?**

Angling is one of the few sports, if not the only one, that has its rules and code of conduct based upon an Act of Parliament – the Salmon and Freshwater Fisheries Act, 1975. The Act is intended to give protection to a resource that is vulnerable and liable to overexploitation if not properly controlled.

To accomplish this the Act caters for the appointment of water bailiffs to enforce its provisions and gives them specific powers to enable them to carry out their duty effectively.

**What are the powers of a water bailiff?**

The powers of a water bailiff are set out in Sections 31 to 36 of the Act. These can be summarised as follows:

(a) he may examine dams, fixed engines, obstructions, etc. and for that purpose enter on to any land;

(b) he may examine any instrument or bait that he has reasonable cause to suspect of being used in taking fish in contravention of the Act and any container he suspects of having been or being used, or likely to be used, for holding any such instrument, bait or fish;

(c) he may stop and search any boat or vessel used in fishing, or any vessel or vehicle that he suspects of containing any fish caught, or instrument, bait or container used in contravention of the Act;

(d) he may seize any fish, instrument, vessel, vehicle or other thing liable to be forfeited under the Act;

(e) he may enter upon and traverse any land adjoining or near to waters in order to prevent an offence against the Act;

(f) he may obtain a warrant to enter and remain upon any land or to search suspected premises;

(g) he can arrest anyone fishing illegally at night;

(h) he may require a person to produce his licence and to give his name and address.

In addition, he is deemed to be a constable for the purpose of enforcing the Act and thereby has certain powers under the Police and Criminal Evidence Act, 1984.

## How can an angler ensure that a person claiming to be a water bailiff is telling the truth?

In some water authority areas the water bailiffs are issued with a distinctive uniform, while in others they go about their duties in civilian clothes. However, whether in uniform or not, a water bailiff who purports to carry out his duty should always produce his warrant as proof of his identity and position.

The format of warrants varies – depending upon the issuing authority – but whatever form it takes the following information should be included:

(a) the name of the water authority;

(b) reference to the Salmon and Freshwater Fisheries Act, 1975;

(c) a statement to the effect that "John Smith is appointed a water bailiff and empowered to enforce the provisions of the above Act";

(d) signature of the issuing officer.

## What happens if an angler is obstructive and refuses to give a water bailiff his name and address or to allow a search?

The Act empowers a water bailiff to require a person who is fishing, or whom he reasonably suspects of being about to fish or to have fished within the preceding half hour, to produce his licence and to state his name and address. To fail to do either is an offence and carries a maximum penalty of £1,000.

If the water bailiff suspects that the person does not have a licence and the latter refuses to give his name and address, the water bailiff can exercise his powers of a constable given under Section 36 of the Act. This means that he can then apply part of the Police and Criminal Evidence Act, 1984 which gives him the power to arrest any person who he reasonably suspects of committing, or having committed, an offence under the 1975 Act, *if*:

(a) the name and address of the person is not known and cannot be readily ascertained; or

(b) the person fails to give a satisfactory address at which a summons can be served; or

(c) the water bailiff has reasonable grounds for doubting that:
   (i) the name furnished is his real name, or
   (ii) the address furnished is a satisfactory address at which a summons can be served.

If the person refuses to allow the water bailiff to make a search, which he is entitled to do under Section 31 of the '75 Act, he has committed another offence which also carries a maximum penalty of £1,000 and for which he could be arrested if he fails to give his name and address.

When making an arrest reasonable force may be used in order to effect it, and the arrested person can be searched for anything relevant to the offence.

A person giving a name and address will be expected to supply documentary or personal confirmation of his identity and will be given ample opportunity to do so before further steps are taken.

## What kind of proof about a person's true identity will a water bailiff accept?

The fishing licence on its own does not necessarily prove that the individual producing it is the person to whom it was issued or whose name appears on it. (The licence could have been stolen or the person using it could have found it at the waterside.)

If a water bailiff has his doubts, or no licence is produced, he will ask for further evidence, such as a driving licence, D.H.S.S. benefit book, personal letters bearing the person's name and address or any other documents of a personal nature. A cheque book bearing the account holder's name would not normally be accepted on its own – it would not give details of the person's address.

Identification by a third person may be acceptable provided that it can be made independently. The mutual identification of two suspects sitting side by side on a river bank is unlikely to be accepted unless supported by some other evidence.

## Can a water bailiff stop anyone from fishing?

If an angler does not have a licence, the water bailiff can require him to stop fishing until he purchases one. A person fishing on private water with a licence but without permission (unless it be on a water authority fishery) cannot be asked to move by a water bailiff – but the bailiff may report him to the fishery owner.

## What can a water bailiff seize from an angler?

If the angler was fishing illegally, his rod, line, reel, terminal tackle, illegal bait, and any fish in his possession at the time would be subject to seizure. If the bait was in a container or the angler had attempted to conceal a fish, e.g. in a sack, that, too, could be seized. If fish scales on clothing are thought to be relevant to the incident, the item of clothing could be seized for forensic examination. In fact, anything which is relevant to the offence may be seized.

It should be borne in mind that a rod and line being used by an angler who does not possess a valid fishing licence is illegal and can be seized.

## What safeguard does an angler have that anything seized from him by a water bailiff can be claimed at a later date?

Whenever anything is seized by a water bailiff he will issue the person from whom it is seized with a receipt listing all items. If a bailiff does not offer a receipt insist on his issuing one.

Never hand over any tackle, fish or other item to anyone unless he can provide evidence, in the form of a warrant or authority from an employer, of his identity and status.

However, under the Theft Act any member of the public can seize anything used in committing an offence under that Act (*see page 39*) and such a person may have no written form of authority. In such a case it is preferable for the angler to accompany the person to a police station and to hand over anything liable to seizure in the presence of a police officer.

## If a rod is seized and subsequently returned in a damaged condition, what can an angler do about it?

The safe custody of anything seized is the responsibility of the person seizing it and if it is later returned in a damaged condition a claim can be made against him. It is for this reason that a water bailiff will examine closely any item seized and note on the receipt details of any damage observed at the time so that if in future a claim is made evidence as to the state of the item when seized is available.

## If a water bailiff seizes anything from an angler, will he get it back later?

If it is decided that no proceedings will be taken against him, anything seized will be returned.

If it is decided to prosecute, the items seized will be retained and produced when the case comes to court. Items seized but not required as evidence should be returned to their owner as soon as possible.

If the court finds the defendant guilty, it can make an order of forfeiture for all or some of the items seized. This means that the angler will not get those items back.

If a court makes such an order, it is usually only in respect of the actual instrument used in the offence and any fish taken. Other seized items would be returned.

A fish, such as a salmon, which is seized can either be preserved for presentation in court as evidence or sold (provided it is in season and not unclean or immature) and the proceeds of the sale held until the case is heard. If the defendant is found not guilty, he will have the fish, or the proceeds of the sale, returned to him. If not, the fish or the money could be the subject of a forfeiture order.

## Under what circumstances can a water bailiff seize a car?

For an offence involving prohibited instruments or fishing without a licence – but not for angling without a licence – when the offender could be indicted to be tried by a crown court. However, if an angler visited a river by car and then decided to try and take fish by any method other than by conventional angling, and was caught, he could find himself faced with a long walk home!

## What about seizing a boat?

The same circumstances apply as for a car. If any offence committed relates only to the conventional use of a rod and line, the boat cannot be seized.

## If someone is seen taking a fish illegally and then running into a house, what can a water bailiff do about it?

Although his powers do not give him an automatic right of access to a dwelling house, or the curtilage of a dwelling house, he can, when he has good reason to suspect that fish have been illegally taken or illegal nets or other instruments are on the property, apply to a Justice of the Peace for a warrant under Section 33 of the Act. If it is granted, it gives him the power to enter and search the property. This warrant remains effective for up to a week, after which a new one must be applied for if the first one has not been used.

Access to certain land such as decoys, or land used for the preservation of wild fowl, is denied to a water bailiff under normal circumstances but again, should the need arise, he can apply to a Justice of the Peace for an order authorising him to enter and remain on the land for up to twenty-four hours.

## If caught breaking the law, what advice should an angler be given?

To avoid making the situation any worse he should do nothing that will give rise to the committing of another offence. He should keep cool and cooperate as fully as he is legally obliged to, with the water bailiff giving him all the details he requires, and he should hand over any items that the water bailiff wants to seize.

Giving a wrong name and/or address and refusing to hand over anything liable to seizure are additional offences – the first can lead to arrest.

The bailiff will caution the suspect and give him the opportunity to make a statement. If he has a valid excuse he should give it at this stage, as this, if it can be checked, may establish his innocence and result in no further action being taken. The statement can be quite simple and consist of just a few words – in which case the water bailiff will write it in his notebook and ask the angler to sign it – or it can be much longer, especially if the circumstances merit it, when what is said will be recorded on a separate form. The angler will be given the opportunity of writing this himself or dictating it to the water bailiff. When the statement is complete the angler should read it through and insist that any amendments, deletions or additions are recorded and initialled before finally signing it.

# 15
# Legal proceedings

**What happens if it is decided to prosecute for a fishing offence?**

All fishery offences are dealt with initially by a magistrates' court and it is before such that the person prosecuted is required to appear.

He will be notified of the charge or charges made against him by means of a summons, which requires him to present himself at the court, on a date and at the time shown, in order to answer them. This is an order of the court and must be obeyed. The summons may be sent to him by recorded delivery post or served on him personally by a water bailiff or police officer.

The court may use the Magistrates' Court Act procedure whereby, in addition to the summons, the defendant is sent the following documents:

1. an explanatory statement setting out his options, viz. that he can:
   (a) plead "Guilty" on the appropriate form and not appear in court
   (b) appear in court and plead "Guilty"
   (c) appear in court and plead "Not guilty".

If he does not reply to the summons, the court could hear the case in his absence;

2. a statement of facts – this is the evidence against him and is the only evidence that the court would allow in his absence;

3. a form on which to plead "Guilty" and set out any mitigating circumstances;

4. a form on which to acknowledge the receipt of the summons;

5. a list of any previous convictions to which it is intended to draw the attention of the court. (Previous convictions cannot be quoted unless this has been sent or the defendant appears in court in person.)

## What should an individual do on receiving a summons?

He should read it thoroughly, especially the offence or offences with which he is charged and, when the Magistrates' Court Act procedure is used, the statement of facts. If both correspond with what occurred (and in the great majority of cases the individual is fully aware that he has committed the offence or offences), he will probably save himself a lot of time and money by pleading "Guilty". He can do this either by letter or by completing the forms sent to him under the Magistrates' Court Act procedure and sending them to the clerk of the court. A written apology giving details of any extenuating circumstances should be included – this may sway the decision of the court in the angler's favour by lessening the severity of the penalty.

There is nothing to prevent someone appearing in court and pleading "Guilty" in person. Some courts regard this as a courtesy which may have a beneficial effect upon the outcome.

If an individual wishes to dispute the charges or the statement of facts by pleading "Not guilty", he would be well advised to seek legal advice, especially if the alleged offence is of a serious nature carrying a high penalty.

## What happens in the court?

Every court that deals with criminal cases adheres to the same general procedure which has been established for many years. Under this both the defendant and the prosecution are given equal opportunities to present their case and to question the evidence of the other side.

The evidence is heard by magistrates (also called the bench) in the magistrates' court and by a judge and jury in the higher court.

The work of the court is controlled by its clerk whose duty is to ensure that the correct procedures are followed and that no injustices occur. To this end he will assist anyone who is not represented by a solicitor to present his case in the approved way.

If the defendant pleads "Guilty", the position is much simplified and the usual procedure is for the prosecuting solicitor to read out the statement of facts and, if the defendant is present, a list of any previous convictions. In the event of the defendant pleading "Guilty" by post these can only be quoted if he has been previously notified in writing of the intention to do so. When the court has heard the evidence it decides upon an appropriate penalty and announces this.

If the defendant pleads "Not guilty", the prosecution outlines the circumstances and then calls its witnesses to give their evidence on oath. The defendant or his solicitor can then cross-examine each witness.

When the prosecution has finished, the defendant can say nothing, make a statement or give evidence on oath and can call witnesses to verify his evidence or support his case. If the defendant or any witnesses he calls give evidence on oath, they can be cross-examined by the prosecution. When both sides have finished giving their evidence the bench retires to consider the facts and to reach a verdict.

When the bench returns to the courtroom the verdict of "Guilty" or "Not guilty" is announced. In the latter case the defendant is free to leave the court without a stain on his character. If a "Guilty" verdict is found, the bench will ask whether the defendant has any previous convictions and if so these will be read out. It will then ask the defendant if he has anything to say by way of mitigation – this gives him the opportunity to express his regrets for the offence and to proffer his apologies to all concerned! The bench may question him about his financial status, e.g. how much he earns, what rent he pays, etc. When satisfied that it has all the relevant information, the bench confers to decide on a suitable penalty which it then announces. If a fine is imposed, the defendant may be given time in which to pay it off. The bench may also make an order for the confiscation of any fish or instrument involved in the case.

## Apart from a fine, what other penalties can a court impose?

Under the Salmon Act, 1986, a magistrates' court can impose a prison sentence of up to three months for certain offences under the 1975 Act. It can also cause other serious offences under the 1975 Act to be referred to the crown court for trial, or sentence, where the penalty can be imprisonment for up to two years, an unspecified fine, or both.

The courts can give the offender a conditional discharge, too, which means that, although no other penalty is imposed at this time, if the defendant appears later in any court for some other offence the circumstances under which the conditional discharge was made can be taken into account when passing sentence for the second offence.

Where the case is proved, but the nature of the offence is such that the court feels no penalty is called for, it can give the offender an absolute discharge. This is a conviction and should not be regarded as exonerating its recipient.

Where the court is of the opinion that neither imprisonment nor a fine is appropriate, it has the power to sentence an offender to community service, whereby he is required to carry out a specified number of hours' work for the benefit of the community under the supervision of an approved person.

The court can also order the offender to contribute to the cost of bringing the case – even if no fine is imposed.

## If a person feels he has been wrongly convicted, what can he do?

Under certain circumstances an individual can appeal to a superior court, but this is a matter that must be discussed and considered in consultation with a solicitor.

## Is there anything else an angler should know about legal proceedings?

The above questions obviously deal with the subject in a very cursory way and are intended merely to give a guide to what is involved. The procedures are set out in detail in *Stone's Justices' Manual* – the clerks' to the courts Bible – and anyone *really* interested in the subject should read it. An alternative would be to visit a local court and see at first hand the law in action.

# Endpiece

The foregoing sets out in relatively simple terms the law as it applies to the questions asked, but the reader must be careful not to interpret this as the definitive solution to every seemingly similar situation. In all matters relating to the law the final arbiter which can decide upon the merits of a case is a court – which has the power to punish offenders under the criminal law and to rectify the wrongs suffered by a person under the civil law – but prior to this lawyers can explain the legal position and give an opinion on the facts as presented and the likely outcome of a court case.

This book has attempted to prevent the angler falling foul of the law by drawing his attention to the legislation and to common law as it affects his sport. It is not intended to replace a qualified legal expert who should always be consulted if a matter is of sufficient seriousness to warrant it.

# Appendix A

**Summary of the Salmon and Freshwater Fisheries Act, 1975**

Part 1
(Prohibition of certain modes of taking or destroying fish)

Section  1   Prohibited implements
Section  2   Roe, spawning and unclean fish, etc.
Section  3   Nets
Section  4   Poisonous matter and polluting effluent
Section  5   Prohibition of use of explosives, poisons or electrical devices and of destructions of dams, etc.


Part 2
(Obstructions to passage of fish)

Section  6   Fixed engines
Section  7   Fishing weirs
Section  8   Fishing mill dams
Section  9   Duty to make and maintain fish passes
Section 10   Power of water authority to construct and alter fish passes
Section 11   Ministers' consents and approvals for fish passes
Section 12   Penalty for injuring or obstructing fish pass or gap
Section 13   Sluices
Section 14   Gratings
Section 15   Power of water authority to use gratings, etc. to limit movement of salmon and trout
Section 16   Boxes and cribs in weirs and dams

Part 6
(Miscellaneous and supplementary)

Section 38   Works below high water mark
Section 39   Border rivers and Solway Firth
Section 40   River Severn
Section 41   Interpretation
Section 42   Repeals, etc.
Section 43   Citation etc.

Schedule 1
(Close seasons and close times)

Schedule 2
(Licences)

Schedule 3
(Administration)
Part 1 – Orders
Part 2 – Byelaws
Part 3 – Miscellaneous

Schedule 4
(Offences)
Part 1 – Prosecution and punishment
Part 2 – Procedure

Schedule 5
(Repeals)

# Appendix B

EXAMPLES OF BYELAWS APPLYING TO ANGLING MADE BY WATER
AUTHORITIES

## Fixing or altering the close seasons

The annual close season for freshwater fish in waters within the area
shall be from 28 February to the following 31 May, both dates
inclusive. (*Yorkshire Water Authority, Byelaw 2*)

The annual close season for fishing for non-migratory trout with
rod and line shall be from 1 October to the following 24 March, both
dates inclusive. (*Yorkshire Water Authority, Byelaw 3*)

The annual close season for fishing for brown (non-migratory)
trout with rod and line shall be the period from and including the 1st
day of October to and including the 14th day of March following.
(*North West Water Authority, Byelaw 4*)

## Dispensing with the close season for freshwater fish or rainbow trout

There shall be no annual close season for freshwater fish in the Area.
(*South West Water Authority (Cornwall River Authority, Byelaw
32)*)

The annual close season for fishing for rainbow trout with a rod
and line in all waters in the Water Authority area shall be dispensed
with. (*Severn Trent Water Authority, Byelaw 3(d)(ii)*)

The annual close season for fishing for rainbow trout with rod and line shall be dispensed with for enclosed waters. (*Anglian Water Authority, Byelaw 3*)

## Specifying nets which may be used, including keep nets

(i) No person shall use a keep-net for retaining any kind of fish during the annual close season for freshwater fish.

(ii) No person shall after 15 June 1984 use a keep-net;

(a) of less than 2.0 metres in extended length;

(b) with rings less than 380 mm in diameter or, if rectangular, less than 355 mm by 255 mm;

(c) with wider spacing of rings than one ring per 300 mm, excluding the top ring;

(d) with a mesh size of more than 16 mm, measured diagonally from knot to knot when stretched and wet.

(iii) The use of keep nets commonly known as "micromesh" nets is permitted. In the case of such nets the width of the mesh measured when wet but unstretched shall not exceed 8 mm and such nets shall comply with (ii)(a), (b) and (c) above. (*North West Water Authority, Byelaw 18*)

## Prohibiting the use and time of use of certain instruments

No person shall fish with more than one rod and line at a time for salmon and trout (including rainbow trout) or with more than two rods and lines at a time for freshwater fish and eels. (*Welsh Water Authority, Byelaw 12*)

No person shall use or attempt to use any night hook, fixed hook, night line, hand line or fixed line for taking salmon, trout or freshwater fish within the Area. (*South West Water Authority (Cornwall River Authority, Byelaw 25)*)

No person shall use in fishing for salmon or migratory trout in the Area any instrument other than a net of the type specified in Byelaw 7 (Kinds of Nets), a fixed engine lawfully used or a rod and line. (*South West Water Authority (Devon River Authority, Byelaw 45)*)

## Prohibiting the taking or removal of any fish whether alive or dead from any waters

No person (other than a Water Bailiff of the Authority acting in his offical capacity) shall take or remove any live fish or any dead fish from any waters within the Authority's area, except in accordance with the written authority of the Authority or unless otherwise he is lawfully authorised so to do. (*Welsh Water Authority, Byelaw 8*)

No person may take or remove from any waters within the area of the Authority without lawful authority any fish, whether dead or alive. (*North West Water Authority, Byelaw 15*)

## Prohibiting or regulating the taking of trout or any freshwater fish of a size less than that as may be prescribed by the byelaw

No person shall take away from any waters within the area any fish of a kind and of a size less than such as is hereinafter prescribed, that is to say:

| | | | |
|---|---|---|---|
| Barbel | 40 cm | Gudgeon | 13 cm |
| Bleak | 10 cm | Perch | 22 cm |
| Bream | 30 cm | Pike | 60 cm |
| Carp | 30 cm | Roach | 18 cm |
| Crucian Carp | 18 cm | Rudd | 20 cm |
| Chub | 30 cm | Tench | 25 cm |
| Dace | 15 cm | Brown Trout | 25 cm |
| Grayling | 25 cm | | |

The size shall be ascertained by measuring from the tip of the snout to the end of the tail fin. Provided that this byelaw shall not apply to any person who:

(i) takes any undersized fish if the same is kept alive in a keep-net and returned alive to the water at the point of capture not later than at the conclusion of fishing;

(ii) takes any undersized freshwater fish (not exceeding twelve in one day) for use as bait in the water from which they were taken;

(iii) takes any undersized fish for any specific purpose with the previous consent in writing of the authority. (*Thames Water Authority, Byelaw 8*)

## Prohibiting or regulating the taking of fish above or below any dam or other obstruction

No person shall take or attempt to take, by any means, salmon, trout or freshwater fish or eels within a distance of 15 metres above and 45 metres below or downstream of the crest of Shrewsbury Weir. (*Severn Trent Water Authority, Byelaw 16(a)*)

No person shall take or attempt to take by any means any fish in any waters within a distance of 50 yards below the crest of Kilbury Weir on the River Dart. (*South West Water Authority (Devon River Authority, Byelaw 43)*)

## Prohibiting or regulating fishing with rod and line during the hours of darkness

No person shall fish for, take or kill any salmon, trout or freshwater fish with rod and line in the River Esk between the downstream side of Ruswarp Road Bridge and the Whitby harbour mouth between the expiration of the first hour after sunset on any day and the beginning of the last hour before sunrise on the following morning during the months of September and October in any year. (*Yorkshire Water Authority, Byelaw 12*)

## Requiring anglers to submit details of fish caught

Any person fishing for salmon or migratory trout to whom a licence is issued by the Authority shall immediately upon the expiration of the period of the licence make a full and true return to the Authority on a form contained in the licence, of the location and of the date on which any salmon or migratory trout were taken and the number and weight of all such salmon or migratory trout taken, or a statement that the person had taken no such fish. (*Welsh Water Authority, Byelaw 11*)

(i) Any person who takes salmon or migratory trout by rod and line within the area shall make a full return to the Authority of the number, length, weight and place of capture of salmon or migratory trout before the last day of November in any year;

(ii) except with the previous written consent of the Authority any person who takes a zander by rod and line or by any other approved method of fish removal within the area shall, within fourteen days of the taking thereof, make a written return to the Authority of the number and place of capture and shall thereafter give such other particulars as the Authority may reasonably require. (*Thames Water Authority, Byelaw 15*)

## Regulating the use of any lure or bait used in connection with fishing with rod and line

No person shall:

(a) in fishing with rod and line for salmon in the Severn area use any float in conjunction with any lure or bait;

(b) in fishing with rod and line during the annual close season for freshwater fish, use any float or bait (including groundbait) other than artificial or natural fly, spinners, minnows or worms. (*Severn Trent Water Authority, Byelaw 11*)

No person shall, except as in hereafter provided, use in fishing for salmon or trout a worm baited on more than a single hook and such hook shall not exceed 40 mm in length overall nor 15 mm in width of gape and the weight or weights used to sink the hook shall not in any case exceed 30 g in the aggregate; provided that a tackle of two or three hooks may be used if tied one above the other upon a single strand of gut or other artificial substitute material, and if each of such hooks does not exceed 15 mm in length and is not more than 8 mm in width of gape. (*North West Water Authority, Byelaw 20*)

## Determining a time when the use of a gaff shall be lawful

During the months of February, March, April and October in each year no person shall use a gaff in connection with fishing with rod and line in any waters within the Area other than landlocked lakes and ponds. (*Northumbrian Water Authority, Byelaw 19*)

It shall be lawful to use a gaff in connection with fishing with rod and line for salmon or migratory trout in the Avon and Dorset

Division between the first day after the end of the appropriate close season and the 31st day of August following. (*Wessex Water Authority, Byelaw 18*)

## Authorising the fishing for eels during the annual close season for freshwater fish

Fishing for eels during the annual close season for freshwater fish shall be permitted in the tidal River Thames downstream of the Thames Barrier. (*Thames Water Authority, Byelaw 7*)

It shall be lawful to fish for eels with a rod and line during the annual close season for freshwater fish in the Water Authority area. (*Severn Trent Water Authority, Byelaw 3(e)*)

## For the better execution of the Act and the better protection, preservation and improvement of the fisheries in a water authority area

All salmon and migratory trout hooked otherwise than in the mouth shall be returned to the water without delay and with as little injury as possible. (*Welsh Water Authority, Byelaw 10(b)(2)*)

With the exception of trout, eels and zander, no person without the previous consent in writing of the Authority when fishing with rod and line shall take away from any waters within the area in any one day more than two fish, of which not more than one may be tench, carp, barbel, bream or pike, provided that this byelaw shall not apply to any enclosed reservoir, lake or pond into which or from which fish cannot normally swim from or to other waters. (*Thames Water Authority, Byelaw 9*)

No person shall introduce, or have in his possession intending to introduce, any live or dead fish or spawn thereof or natural food of fish (other than bait) from any source into any waters within the Water Authority areas or transfer any fish (including fish for use as live-bait) or spawn thereof or natural food of fish from one water to another within the Water Authority area without the previous consent in writing of, and subject to such conditions as may be imposed by, the Water Authority. (*Severn Trent Water Authority, Byelaw 13*)

# Appendix C

## Useful addresses

### Addresses of water authorities

*Anglian Water Authority*
Ambury House
Huntingdon
Cambs   PE18 6NZ

Tel: (0480) 56181

*Northumbrian Water Authority*
Northumbria House
P.O. Box 4
Regent Centre
Gosforth
Newcastle upon Tyne
NE3 3PX

Tel: (091) 284 3151

*North West Water Authority*
Dawson House
Great Sankey
Warrington   WA5 3LW

Tel: (092 572) 4321

*Severn Trent Water Authority*
Abelson House
2297 Coventry Road
Sheldon
Birmingham   B26 3PU

Tel: (021) 743 4222

*Southern Water Authority*
Guildbourne House
Worthing
West Sussex   BN11 1LD

Tel: (0903) 205252

*South West Water Authority*
Peninsula House
Rydon Lane
Exeter   EX2 7HR

Tel: (0392) 219666

*Thames Water Authority*
Nugent House
Vastern Road
Reading
Berkshire   RG1 8DB

Tel: (0734) 593333

*Welsh Water Authority*
Cambrian Way
Brecon
Powys   LD3 7HP

Tel: (0874) 3181

*Wessex Water Authority*
Wessex House

Passage Street
Bristol   BS2 0JQ

Tel: (0272) 290611

*Yorkshire Water Authority*
21, Park Square South
Leeds
West Yorkshire   LS1 2QG

Tel: (0532) 440191

Copies of the Byelaws currently
in force for the respective areas
can be obtained from the above
addresses.

## Other useful addresses

*Anglers' Cooperative
Association*
Midland Bank Chambers
Westgate
Grantham
Lincolnshire   NH31 6CE

Tel: (0476) 61008

*Institute of Fisheries
Management*
"Balmaha"
Coldwells Road
Holmer
Hereford

Tel: (0437) 6225

*Salmon and Trout Association*
Fishmongers Hall
London Bridge
London   EC4R 9EL

Tel: (01) 283 5838

# Index